How to Survive the SAT [and ACT]

WARNING:

This guide contains differing
opinions. Hundreds of heads will
not always agree. Advice taken in
combination may cause unwanted
side effects. Use your head when
selecting advice.

How to Survive the SAT [and ACT]

by **Hundreds** of College Students Who Did

JAY BRODY, SPECIAL EDITOR

Hundreds of Heads Books, LLC

ATLANTA

Cover photograph by TriggPhoto (left man, right woman), Justin Horrocks (center woman/man) Cover and book design by Elizabeth Johnsboen

Library of Congress Cataloging-in-Publication Data

How to survive the SAT (and ACT) : by hundreds of college students who did / Jay Brody, special editor.
      p. cm.
  ISBN-13: 978-1-933512-06-8
  1. SAT (Educational test) 2. American College Testing Program. 3. Universities and colleges--United States--Entrance examinations. I. Brody, Jay.
  LB2353.57.H59 2007
  378.1'662--dc22

                              2007016695

See pages 211 for credits and permissions.

HUNDREDS OF HEADS® books are available at special discounts when purchased in bulk for premiums or institutional or educational use. Excerpts and custom editions can be created for specific uses. For more information, please e-mail sales@hundredsofheads.com or write to:

HUNDREDS OF HEADS BOOKS, LLC
#230
2221 Peachtree Road, Suite D
Atlanta, Georgia 30309

ISBN-10: 1-933512-06-7
ISBN-13: 978-1933512-06-8

Printed in U.S.A.
10 9 8 7 6 5 4 3 2 1

CONTENTS

THE HEADS EXPLAINED

With hundreds of tips, stories, and advice in this book, how can you quickly find those golden nuggets of wisdom? Of course, we recommend reading the entire book, but you can also look for these special symbols:

 Remember this significant story or advice.

 This may be something to explore in more detail.

Watch out! Be careful! (Can we make it any clearer?)

 We are astounded, thrilled, or delighted by this one.

Here's something to think about.

—*THE EDITOR*
AND HUNDREDS OF HEADS BOOKS

Introduction

As the owner of a test prep firm, I've helped hundreds of kids prepare for the SAT (and the ACT). We spend a lot of time working on the test basics: geometry, vocabulary words, reading comprehension, and so forth. These content areas are important, and studying them is an essential part of getting ready for the test.

However, over the years I've learned that getting ready for the SAT is about much more than being prepared to answer questions about reading, writing, and arithmetic. Sure, good SAT prep includes the legendary strategic aspects of the test: when to guess, how to manage time, and strategic ways to answer difficult questions. But there's also a big psychological component to the SAT—every student brings a different set of expectations to the test, and understanding and managing those expectations is critical.

Each student also has dozens of logistical questions that need to be answered. Should you sacrifice homework time to prepare for the SAT? Is it useful to drink coffee on the morning of the exam? What type of calculator is best? Are SAT classes worth the money? What's the best way to deal with test-day jitters? What's the best time of the year to take the SAT or ACT? What score do you need to get into a good (or decent) college?

These questions don't always have right or wrong answers. And you won't necessarily get the advice that works best for you by picking out an SAT prep guide at the bookstore. Lots of times, the best way to get advice about the SAT—or advice about anything in life, really—is to ask around and take advantage of the experiences of those who came before you.

Sometimes I have students who have older siblings or friends (perhaps ones I also tutored), and I'm usually impressed with how knowledgeable about the SAT the younger students have become. Few kids spend their free time discussing the Pythagorean Theorem or the particulars of subject-verb agreement, but the important stuff gets through. On everything from dealing with the stress of the test to how to study with friends, there are important lessons students learn from their peers that I just can't credibly teach; I often wish that every student could spend at least a few hours getting advice from seniors or recent graduates who have recently done well on the SAT.

That's the idea of this book. On subjects from essay-writing to guessing strategy to dealing with parents, we've collected the advice of hundreds of recent high school graduates who successfully navigated the SAT and the ACT. They dish on everything, including some things your tutors and test prep books aren't allowed to talk about. It's like having hundreds of smart, older friends at your disposal, helping guide you through one of high school's most difficult ordeals.

Read the advice we've assembled here and you'll learn a great deal about what it takes to successfully navigate what's been called the grand-daddy of all admissions tests.

We hope this book can be a great help as you take this crucial step towards a successful college experience. Good luck!

—JAY BRODY

A Rite of Passage: The SAT & You

Someday, you'll look back on the SAT as simply another stepping stone in your 17+ years of formal education. You'll view the test as part of being a teenager and an experience that, while stressful, made you a better person. Yes, there will be a day when the SAT will be a mere blip in your rearview mirror, and you'll feel relief and gratitude that you've moved on to bigger and more important things.

Today is not that day.

If you're reading this book then the SAT is coming up, maybe quickly, and you're about to face one of the most important tests you'll ever encounter. The SAT wasn't designed to add stress to your already *busy life, but sometimes it seems that way. How are you supposed to keep everything in perspective while everyone seems to have gone SAT crazy?*

It helps to take a step back and put everything in perspective. Yes, this is an important test. Yes, it plays a role in the college admissions process. But it's not the be-all and end-all of your high school career.

We asked students to describe the most interesting, disturbing, and memorable parts of their SAT experience. We also asked them to give their opinions about what the SAT does—and doesn't—mean about your intelligence, future, and opportunities for success in the "real world." Their answers may surprise you.

DURING SAT SEASON, you will look (and be) tired, cranky and overworked. Use that to your advantage. Make your sister turn off that god-awful reality show. Put off cleaning your room for an entire month. The sky's the limit.

—*JAWON LEE*
SAN DIEGO, CALIFORNIA
SAT/ACT SCORES: 2400

• • • • • • • •

THE ABILITY TO PLAN AHEAD for studying for the SAT is a strong indicator of how you'll do in college.

—*TIMOTHY MICHAEL COOPER*
NEW YORK, NEW YORK
YALE UNIVERSITY

• • • • • • • •

I DO NOT THINK THE SAT questions necessarily prepare you for college or real life, but the SAT does help you hone certain skills you need in real life—managing pressure, dealing with stress, and preparing for the test with seriousness and maturity.

—*DREW SILVERMAN*
ELKINS PARK, PENNSYLVANIA
SAT/ACT SCORES: 1410
SYRACUSE UNIVERSITY

• • • • • • • •

THE SAT CAN BE LEARNED, just like Spanish or algebra. When you think about it, the SAT only asks about 15 different types of questions in each section, just in different ways. This is especially true of the Math section, where the only difference is the numbers they use. But if you just memorize the different question types along with a little vocabulary, anyone who is self-motivated enough can come close to acing the test.

—*SHARON*
LOS ANGELES, CALIFORNIA
SAT/ACT SCORES: 2190/31
UNDECIDED

Some people do poorly, and some do well. But 10 years from now, you won't even remember your test score, and employers won't ask.

—*BRIAN STANLEY*
CHICAGO, ILLINOIS
SAT/ACT SCORES: 22
ROBERT MORRIS COLLEGE

HEADLINES
Best Advice and Top Tips

- Remember, the SAT is not everything—but by some estimates it counts for a little over a third of your college admissions application.
- Treat the SAT like a triathlon—you need to train in all areas to do well!

SATs DO NOT PROPERLY reflect one's intellectual capabilities. They are only geared for a certain type of brain. It is true that smart people score high on the SATs but there are other equally brilliant students who score quite low.

—*ELANA JUDITH SYRTASH*
NEW YORK, NEW YORK
YESHIVA UNIVERSITY

• • • • • • • •

I KNEW THAT IT WAS IMPORTANT that I get a good score and I did everything I could to prepare. But I also knew that it was necessary for me to have good grades, extracurricular activities, essays, and interview, and I focused on those as well. In the end, I scored lower than some of my classmates on the SAT, but I got into several schools that they didn't.

—*BLAYNE ALEXANDER*
EDMOND, OKLAHOMA
DUKE UNIVERSITY

I DON'T THINK THE **SAT** prepared me for anything. To me, it's just another test. I hardly had a second thought after I was done. The SAT was just something I was hoping do well on to get me into school.

—ERIC GOULD
CHESHIRE, CONNECTICUT
SAT/ACT SCORES: 1050
HOFSTRA UNIVERSITY

. . . .

" The only people in college who will care about your SAT score are your admissions officers, and their opinions cease to matter once your freshman year starts. "

—JAWON LEE
SAN DIEGO, CALIFORNIA
SAT/ACT SCORES: 2400

. . . .

THE **SAT** WAS A CULMINATION of all of the testing that I received prior to college, but very different from everything that came after. For the SAT, there were a few different types of questions that you could master through practice and memorization. In college, my professors offered me the opportunity to think for myself based on the information provided, and I was graded on creativity and the ability to think outside of a multiple-choice world.

—MERYL BRANCH-MCTIERNAN
BROOKLYN, NEW YORK
SAT/ACT SCORES: 1360
SYRACUSE UNIVERSITY

STANDARDIZED TESTING: Y/N

THE SAT IS THE BEST OPTION, albeit not an ideal one. There needs to be some common benchmark for schools to use as they evaluate students. With grade inflation, easy or difficult teachers, etc., the same grade in the same class at the same school doesn't necessarily mean the same thing. Testing vocabulary is a flaw. I think that it's inherently easy to study for and therefore gives an unfair advantage to those who can afford tutors and have the time to study at their leisure for a big test in addition to schoolwork.

> —*ANONYMOUS*
> *ORADELL, NEW JERSEY*
> *SAT/ACT SCORES: 2350*
> *UNDECIDED*

DO THE BEST THAT YOU CAN ON THE SAT, but realize that other than getting you into college, the SAT is pretty meaningless. In my opinion, it's not an accurate assessment of academic ability. I got about 100 points less the second time I took it, proving that it is not measuring my "scholastic aptitude."

> —*SASHA ROSE BUSSEY*
> *ATLANTA, GEORGIA*
> *SAT/ACT SCORES: 1240*
> *UNIVERSITY OF MIAMI*

I THINK THE SAT IS A GOOD MEASURE of who has the money to prepare for it. I know kids who have been studying since 7th grade with private tutors, and they go to Yale. There are definitely geniuses who can pull it off, but the majority of us aren't, and it's about how much time you put into it.

> —*LINDSAY*
> *LOS ANGELES, CALIFORNIA*
> *SAT/ACT SCORES: 1760*
> *UNIVERSITY OF CALIFORNIA, SANTA BARBARA*

THEY SHOULD HAVE THE SAT as a requirement to get into college, but it should not be so heavily weighted. I believe it should be optional. For example, if you were trying to get into a school and you were just on the edge of their requirements then you could opt to take the SAT, and if you did well they would accept you.

—JOCELYN
BEVERLY HILLS, CALIFORNIA
SAT/ACT SCORES: 1540
UNIVERSITY OF ARIZONA

I DON'T THINK THAT THE SAT is a good tool to measure how smart you are. It took them until last year to remove the analogies, which were obviously biased toward certain ethnicities. I don't think the SAT should be required. I have friends who did terribly on it and who are way smarter than I am. They should test you on the things you are supposed to learn in high school, not whether you can arbitrarily figure out some logic problem. The SAT, historically, is based on intelligence tests that were actually developed here at Stanford, which have since been proven completely ridiculous.

—MIKE MELLENTHIN
MENLO PARK, CALIFORNIA
SAT/ACT SCORES: 2340
STANFORD UNIVERSITY

I LIKE TO THINK OF THE SAT as some sort of physical test. Let's compare it to a triathlon and its three sections. Swimming, running, and biking well are three things that would signify a good athlete. A person who is a great athlete will probably do well in a triathlon, but not always. Some people will never be able to swim well or bike well, no matter how hard they try. Some people may not be great long distant runners, but they may be great sprinters. Maybe they are top gymnasts or baseball players; their talents aren't exactly suited to a triathlon, but they are talented nonetheless. The SAT is much the same.

—JOHN
  VENICE, CALIFORNIA
  SAT/ACT SCORES: 2290
  UNDECIDED

• • • • • • • •

MY JUNIOR YEAR, the SAT was all that I was focused on. In my mind, it seemed like the deciding factor between "likely" and "not likely" at all of the top colleges on my list, and I studied religiously for it. I felt like my entire fate was to be decided when I stepped into the testing room; I could not control my heart rate! Now that I can reflect on it, I see the truth. Of course, the SAT is important and should be prepared for, and of course it makes a difference on college admissions, but it's still just a test.

—JOSEPH ANDA
  LITTLE ROCK, ARKANSAS
  SAT/ACT SCORES: 2300
  UNDECIDED

TEST TIDBIT

About 2.3 million students take the SAT annually. Of those taking the test, 1.5 million are college-bound students.

SAT HISTORY

The SAT, which at the time stood for Scholastic Aptitude Test, was introduced in 1926 to help a group of colleges measure the intelligence of incoming freshmen. The test originally lasted only 97 minutes, although more time was quickly added, and consisted of nine separate subtests.

A few years later the SAT was adopted by Harvard University to help expand enrollment by selecting public school students for a scholarship program. By 1940, all of the Ivy League schools were using the SAT to determine scholarships. At the time—somewhat ironically, given the claims of today's SAT detractors—the SAT was viewed as an equalizer that allowed public school students to compete with their elite private school counterparts.

By the 1950s, the SAT, which originally included logic and IQ problems, had begun to more closely resemble today's exam. In the 1960s, the University of California system required all of its applicants to take the SAT, which eventually led to the adoption of the SAT (or its competitor, the ACT) throughout the country.

In 2005, the SAT underwent its most significant changes in 40 years. A writing section was included, which added a human-graded essay to the exam and raised the highest possible score on the SAT from 1600 to 2400. Analogy questions, perhaps the most famous part of the SAT, were eliminated. Other changes were made as well, including varying the length of reading passages and the elimination of one type of math question.

HOW IMPORTANT IS THE SAT?

While there are no official guidelines for how colleges interpret the SAT, and each school takes its own approach, the vast majority of schools view the SAT as an important tool in evaluating incoming college students. By requiring standardized tests such as the SAT or the ACT, colleges can compare students from different types of high schools and different parts of the country.

Also, the SAT tests some concepts that sometimes aren't an official part of the high school curriculum. Grammar, vocabulary, certain types of math problem solving, and time-pressured reading comprehension are all areas tested on the SAT that students may not be explicitly tested on in high school.

Here's a very rough estimate of how a more exclusive college might weight the various college admissions components:

High School Record	40%
Standardized Test Scores	30%
Activities and Extracurricular Accomplishments	10-20%
Essays	5-10%
Recommendations	5%
Other Factors	0-10%

By the time junior year rolls around, a student can exert the most control over his or her application by focusing on the SAT.

THE SATS DO NOT EVEN COME close to predicting how well you will do in college. I took all honors courses and had a high GPA in high school, and I'm doing even better in college than I did then. But I know others who are struggling in college, even though their SAT scores were through the roof.

—*Julie*
Boston, Massachusetts
SAT/ACT Scores: 1190
University of Connecticut

. . . .

" I don't think the SAT prepared me academically for college. I do think that it taught me about discipline and test-taking skills that I'll need throughout my college career. "

—*Cesar Ocampo*
Monterey Park, California

. . . .

HAVING AN EXPANSIVE VOCABULARY is great for college and for life. Basic math skills will also come in handy. But once you get to college, no one will ever ask or care about what you got on your SATs. And even while you are applying to college, your SAT scores are only one factor in the admissions process. They matter now, but in the grand scheme of things, they're not going to change your life either way.

—*Timothy Michael Cooper*
New York, New York
Yale University

The SAT is just a number. The schools can see the kind of student you are from your grades and activities.

—*WHITNEY*
ST. LOUIS,
MISSOURI
🏛 *WASHINGTON*
UNIVERSITY IN
ST. LOUIS

MOST OF MY FRIENDS HAD private tutors and they all scored better than I did. I studied really hard on my own, but the truth is that the SAT doesn't measure how much you know; it is a barometer of how much money you or your parents can spend on lessons to teach you tricks for taking the test.

—*MOLLY*
LAS VEGAS, NEVADA
🏛 *UNIVERSITY OF ARIZONA*

• • • • • • • •

TAKE IT SERIOUSLY; eat, sleep, breathe it. I didn't: I crammed and I got into good colleges, but no money was offered to me, so I couldn't go unless I wanted my parents and myself to be in debt the rest of our lives. So when you have to choose between studying for the SATs or going out with the most popular boy in school, choose to study. Choosing the date might get you a nice night, but the studying will give you a nice life.

—*ANDREA PARKER*
CHICAGO, ILLINOIS
SAT/ACT SCORES: 890
🏛 *SOUTHERN ILLINOIS UNIVERSITY, CARBONDALE*

MARK YOUR CALENDAR

The SAT is offered at least seven times a year: October, November, December, January, March/April, May, and June.

The ACT is offered six times a year: September, October, December, February, April, and June.

Getting Started: The First Steps to a High Score

So you know the SAT is pretty much unavoidable and you've decided to do whatever you can to help yourself get ready. What should you do first? That depends upon where you are in the process and your college admissions goals (if you have any yet!).

If you're a sophomore, for example, you've got plenty of time. Your first steps will probably be to decide when you'll take your first official SAT (spring of junior year is typically a good time) and decide how you're going to get ready for that test (tutoring, classes, self-study, etc.).

If you're a senior, on the other hand, and you've put off thinking about the SAT until the last minute, your first steps will probably be a little more rushed. Instead of leisurely assembling an SAT calendar, *you'll be planning cram sessions and looking up SAT deadlines at the colleges to which you're applying. Still, you won't be the first one to wait until the last minute to study for the SAT, and all of the best colleges have plenty of students who swear they didn't open up a book until the night before the test.*

We asked recent SAT-takers about their first steps when getting ready for the test. Here's their advice, along with their experiences as they approached the SAT for the first time: the good, the bad, and the ugly.

I TOOK MY FIRST SAT my sophomore year in high school. I just wanted to get in some practice and I wanted to be prepared for when my scores really mattered. I think this really helped me because when I had to take it at the end of my junior year, I knew exactly what to expect.

—*KIRA*
FRESNO, CALIFORNIA
SAT/ACT SCORES: 1340

• • • • • • • •

I STARTED PREPARING for the SAT in 10th grade of high school with the PSAT, and I also took a Princeton Review class the summer before 11th grade. Starting early is key. Don't wait until the last minute to study!

—*ALAINA SILVERMAN*
ELKINS PARK, PENNSYLVANIA
SAT/ACT SCORES: 1210
🏛 *UNIVERSITY OF MARYLAND*

I started studying the summer after sophomore year.

—*JESSICA*
DALLAS, TEXAS
🏛 *RICE UNIVERSITY*

BUT I'M TOO BUSY AT SCHOOL TO FOCUS ON THE SAT!

Love it or hate it, the SAT is a huge part of the admissions process and you need to respect it as such. School is definitely the most important place for you to spend your time, and your grades in school are indeed the most important factor in college admissions. But test scores are a close second, and if you think about it, the time you spend on the SAT should do justice to the test's real importance. Between class time and homework, you'll probably devote at least 6,000 hours to schoolwork during your high school career. Doesn't the SAT warrant at least a good 40-50 hours of study?

HEADLINES
Best Advice and Top Tips

- In the fall of junior year, take the PSAT to see where you stand. In spring of junior year, take the SAT or ACT, or both. You'll have time to take it again, if needed.
- You can't cram for the SAT. Give yourself at least a few months of study time before you take the test.

GET IT OVER WITH YOUR JUNIOR YEAR. Going into your senior year knowing you don't have to take another standardized test is a great feeling.

—*ANONYMOUS*
ST. LOUIS, MISSOURI
WILLIAMS COLLEGE

• • • • • • • •

IT'S A GOOD IDEA TO TAKE the PSAT. I took mine in 10th grade and it really helped me prepare. All of my friends, except for one, did better on the SAT than they did on the PSAT, and I think that it's because the PSAT helps you prepare. The PSAT is very similar in style to the SAT, and you also get the experience of taking the PSAT in the same type of setting and environment that you will later have with the SAT.

—*BURTON DEWITT*
MELVILLE, NEW YORK
SAT/ACT SCORES: 2080/32
RICE UNIVERSITY

I GET REALLY NERVOUS ABOUT TESTS, so taking the SAT my sophomore year helped me relax. I focused on how to take the test and how to handle the pressure. It was amazing how much I learned about my test-taking skills when I was not focused on the grade. When I took the SAT in my junior year, I felt calmer and more confident in my test-taking ability.

—*LAURA BOUTWELL*
WINCHESTER, VIRGINIA
SAT/ACT SCORES: 1410
COLLEGE OF WILLIAM AND MARY

• • • • • • • •

I THINK MOST PEOPLE say to take your SAT at your high school or somewhere familiar, but the opposite worked for me. Having to find the locations and figure things out ensured that I would be wide awake and alert. I know that if I were at my high school, I would have been more tired. Looking at the same walls and the same clocks puts me to sleep.

—*ANONYMOUS*
LAS VEGAS, NEVADA
SAT/ACT SCORES: 2300
VANDERBILT UNIVERSITY

You cannot cram for the SAT. Instead, you must study over a period of time—preferably six months or more.

—*TIMOTHY MICHAEL*
COOPER
NEW YORK,
NEW YORK
YALE
UNIVERSITY

PSAT INFO

How is the PSAT different from the SAT? It's only 2 hours and 10 minutes long, and it has no essay or Algebra II on it.

When is it offered? October. Check with your guidance office for an exact date.

Why take it? It's practice for the SAT, and it's a qualifying test for National Merit Scholarships and Letters of Commendation.

FIVE GOOD REASONS

You should start studying in middle school (which I did) because:

1) In high school you'll have problems balancing your SAT study with the rest of your school life, whereas in middle school you'll have very little studying to do.

2) Any scores you obtain in middle school will only work to your credit (Wow, you're taking the SAT in middle school? You're so smart!). If you score well, so be it. If you score badly, you can expect your scores to increase anyway; no pressure.

3) If you do well on the SAT in middle school, you don't have to worry about it in high school.

4) Even if you do badly, if you work hard you can still boost your grade to a score respectable for a high school student.

5) SAT vocabulary is useful for high school.

—*JESSICA*
BOCA RATON, FLORIDA
SAT/ACT SCORES: 2390
CALIFORNIA INSTITUTE OF TECHNOLOGY

I BOUGHT ONE OF THE SAT study guides about two months before I took it, and I took my SAT early in my senior year. If I had to do it again I would have planned better. I would have bought the book at least six months before I planned to take the SAT and I would have taken it for the first time during my junior year. I barely had enough time to take it for the second time and still get my scores in by the deadline.

—*CODY*
PHOENIX, ARIZONA
SAT/ACT SCORES: 1900
UNIVERSITY OF ARIZONA

WHERE YOU TAKE THE TEST MATTERS! One of my testing sessions was held in a university auditorium, and it was a logistical mess. It took forever for everyone to get seated, get quiet, and get all the papers passed out. If you can schedule it so you can take it at a smaller location it's much less frustrating.

—*LAURA*
CINCINNATI, OHIO
SAT/ACT SCORES: 31
FRANCISCAN UNIVERSITY OF STEUBENVILLE

. . . .

" My mom made me take it in my sophomore year, and I freaked out when I got my score back. But it was a great way to learn what to expect and how to work within the time constraints. "

—*TEKLA TOMAN*
YOUNGSTOWN, OHIO
SAT/ACT SCORES: 29
XAVIER UNIVERSITY

. . . .

KNOW WHAT SCORE RANGE you are aiming for before you take the SAT. Use your PSAT scores as a benchmark to help you set those goals. This will help you determine whether you are satisfied with your score and whether you should take it again. Using PSATs as a standard (as opposed to the SAT range for your dream college) will help you be realistic.

—*S.N.*
RALEIGH, NORTH CAROLINA
SAT/ACT SCORES: 2390

SIGNING UP

SIGN UP EARLY. LOCATION IS SO IMPORTANT, and if you don't sign up early, you may not get to take the test at your first choice. Many of my friends ended up taking the exam at faraway locations. They told me they were uncomfortable, people were cheating left and right, and it was loud. I got to take my exam at Beverly Hills High; it was quiet and I was really comfortable because it was my actual high school.

> —*AARON*
> *BEVERLY HILLS, CALIFORNIA*
> *SAT/ACT SCORES: 2150*
> *UNIVERSITY OF CALIFORNIA, BERKELEY*

• • • • • • • • •

I TOOK THE SAT THREE TIMES, but the second time I took it I ended up canceling my scores mid-test. I didn't like the environment and I kept getting distracted. It was freezing (the proctor told us that the heating system broke down), and I just didn't like the school (it was in a bad part of Sacramento). I learned two things from this experience: 1) Always know what kind of school it is before you sign up for the testing place. 2) Make sure that you take your SAT no later than October. Why? Because even if you cancel your October SAT, you can always take the November one, and if you mess up the November one, you have the December one (the last chance).

> —*JIKYU CHOI*
> *FAIR OAKS, CALIFORNIA*
> *SAT/ACT SCORES: 2370*
> *STANFORD UNIVERSITY*

• • • • • • • • •

I WAS LATE REGISTERING FOR MY SAT, so I had to pay an additional fee to sign up for it. I recommend signing up on time, especially if you are going to take it multiple times. The fees add up!

> —*DILCIA LOOMIS*
> *BUENA PARK, CALIFORNIA*
> *CLAREMONT MCKENNA COLLEGE*

WHEN YOU SIGN UP FOR THE SATs, take advantage of the free score reports, but there is a risk. You can have up to four reports sent out to schools when you apply to take the SAT online, otherwise you have to pay $15 for each report. If you already have a high score and are taking the SAT again, you might want to consider waiting to send your scores. For example, my scores dropped on one of my tests but I already sent my scores. That might have been the reason I didn't get into my early-decision school.

—*CHRIS*
NORTHPORT, NEW YORK
SAT/ACT SCORES: 2180
BOSTON COLLEGE

WHEN TO TAKE IT?

MANY PEOPLE AT MY SCHOOL take the SAT I in April of their junior year, SAT IIs in May, and then take the SAT I again in June if they need to. I think that's really smart because then you're all done before senior year, even if you need to retake it. Getting it done before senior year is a really good idea. The first semester of senior year is more than crazy enough without the SATs hanging over your head.

> —*BECKY*
> *NEWTON, MASSACHUSETTS*
> *SAT/ACT SCORES: 2290*
> *SWARTHMORE COLLEGE*

• • • • • • • • •

TAKE YOUR SAT II SUBJECT TESTS in conjunction with your AP tests, not before and not after, but at the same time. I took the subject test for chemistry in June and I wish I'd taken it in May, when I was taking my AP tests. Originally I thought it would be too much work and preparation to take them all at the same time, but the tests covered the same material. I could have killed two birds with one stone, but instead I had to study like crazy for two tests, on two separate occasions, that were almost alike.

> —*LOUIS S. WU*
> *SILVER SPRING, MARYLAND*
> *SAT/ACT SCORES: 2300*
> *UNIVERSITY OF MARYLAND*

• • • • • • • • •

DON'T WORRY about taking the SAT before January of your junior year, unless it is necessary for some program. If you start before junior year, you will drown in stress because you'll get lower scores than you are capable of. But don't wait until senior year to start testing, or you will drown in stress because you'll have too much work with college applications to complete.

> —*S.N.*
> *RALEIGH, NORTH CAROLINA*
> *SAT/ACT SCORES: 2390*

I **TOOK MY FIRST SAT DURING MY SOPHOMORE YEAR** in high school; I took it once in my junior year and once in my senior year. I spaced out the tests over three years to see if what I learned each year in high school would improve my scores, and it did. I did better each time I took it.

—*SHARLA*
KAUAI, HAWAII
SAT/ACT SCORES: 2000
UNIVERSITY OF SOUTHERN CALIFORNIA

I **TOOK MY FIRST SAT EARLY IN MY JUNIOR YEAR** of high school. Some people thought that was too early, but I think it is a good idea in case you want to take it a few more times. It also leaves you room in case something important, or an emergency, comes up on the day you need to take it. You won't worry as much about missing it.

—*MOLLY*
LAS VEGAS, NEVADA
UNIVERSITY OF ARIZONA

I **TOOK MY FIRST SAT IN SEVENTH GRADE.** A lot of people frown on this but I think it was a great idea. It gives you the opportunity to practice and get comfortable taking standardized tests. The advantage is that the colleges will not look at any test you take before high school. Once you get to high school there is really no such thing as a practice test; they all count.

—*CHRIS*
NORTHPORT, NEW YORK
SAT/ACT SCORES: 2180
BOSTON COLLEGE

SUGGESTED SAT CALENDAR

If you're reading this book as a sophomore or even a junior, you've got time to plan out—yes, and write down!—everything you need to do to get ready for the SAT. Keep a calendar or plan of action, and tack it on the fridge, wall, or bulletin board.

JUNIOR YEAR

- Find out when the PSAT is given at your school and put it on the calendar. If you're a *very good* test taker you might want to prepare for the PSAT, because it's the qualifying test for National Merit scholarships (only relevant for the top few percent of students).
- In the fall or winter, make a decision about whether you want to get a tutor or enroll in a course for the SAT. Note: The best teachers can fill up months in advance, so call in October or November to get into January or February courses.
- Decide whether to take the SAT, ACT, or both.
- Take the test for the first time in the spring (March or May for the SAT, April for the ACT). Put the test date on your calendar, as well as the deadline for signing up for the test.
- Make sure you plan out a study schedule that concludes before you take the exam. If you're taking a class or hiring a tutor, make sure the sessions all finish before the SAT test date.
- If you don't have the score you need for the colleges to which you're applying, take the test again in June.

SENIOR YEAR

- Assess your SAT score in light of where you plan to apply to colleges.
- Reconsider your study plan and consider hiring a tutor or joining a class if you haven't already.
- If necessary, take the test again (and, possibly, again).
- Relax—it's all over!

I WENT TO PENN STATE UNIVERSITY for an SAT prep course the summer of my sophomore year. The course was five and a half weeks long and I lived on campus. To me, it's better if you do something like this during the summer, rather than when you're in school. The prep course was great. It was fun to live on campus and have the experience.

—*BRANDON MALKI*
WEST ORANGE, NEW JERSEY
SAT/ACT SCORES: 1300
BLOOMSBURG UNIVERSITY OF PENNSYLVANIA

I started studying in my first semester, junior year in high school. I bought one of those official SAT study guides and took practice tests.

—*A.C.*
BERKELEY,
CALIFORNIA
SAT/ACT
SCORES: 1800
UNIVERSITY OF
CALIFORNIA,
BERKELEY

I RECOMMEND BUYING PRACTICE SAT books only from the College Board. This isn't because I want the College Board to get more money, but because the other books often have errors or poorly written questions—because they're not taken from real SATs. Do tons of practice questions. Then go over all the answers and figure out why you missed the ones you got wrong. There is no magic bullet; this is the only way to improve at taking the test.

—*TIMOTHY MICHAEL COOPER*
NEW YORK, NEW YORK
YALE UNIVERSITY

I'VE TAKEN MY SATS at four different testing centers and the one closest to my home was the most comfortable. I don't know why, except that maybe being closer to home has some kind of psychological impact. I would have liked to have taken all of the tests at that one testing center, but unfortunately I got a little lazy and ended up registering too late. I tell juniors in my school to plan ahead for the tests.

—*JOON NAM*
MURRIETA, CALIFORNIA
SAT/ACT SCORES: 2220
UNDECIDED

THE BEST WAY TO DO TOP-NOTCH on the SATs is to start studying for it in 7th grade. Get the books, take the classes, and take practice tests every three months. Studying it a year before is like cramming. That's what I did. I got all the books I could on how to score. I scored below average. And even though I was in the top 25 percent of my graduating class and was the editor of my award-winning school newspaper, all the private prestigious colleges saw was a below-average test score, so no scholarship was given to me.

—*ANDREA PARKER*
CHICAGO, ILLINOIS
SAT/ACT SCORES: 890
SOUTHERN ILLINOIS UNIVERSITY, CARBONDALE

BLAME CALIFORNIA!

The University of California made the SAT a requirement for admissions in 1967. As a result, the test was quickly adopted as an admission requirement for universities nationwide.

Hitting the Books: Studying for the Big Test

W hat's the best way to study for the SAT? Everyone has his or her own theory about studying for standardized tests. Some people swear that all you need to do is open a book and go over practice problems for a few hours. Some annoying, near-perfect scorers claim that any studying is a waste of time. Meanwhile, others have rigorous systems of self-study or join study groups with their friends. And although some people hire tutors or enroll in classes that cost "just" a few hundred dollars, there are families that spend thousands and thousands on teachers, tutors, and SAT prep systems.

What should you do? It's a personal choice. But there's a good chance that the same strategies and study habits that work best for you at school will also serve you well while you study for the SAT.

If setting aside a few hours each Saturday afternoon works well before a big math exam, it will probably work well for the SAT. If early in the morning is the best time for you to focus, you should keep that in mind here.

There are of course, some dos and don'ts about studying for any test, and the SAT is no exception. You want to find a quiet place to study and set aside some time when you won't be disturbed. And you need to give yourself enough time before the test to go over all of the material (cramming doesn't work as well for the SAT as it does for, say, a history test).

In this chapter, we asked students for original tips on what worked (and didn't work) for them.

TAKING CARE OF YOURSELF GOES along with studying. Junior year can be the most stressful time of your teenage life, and making sure to stay calm and healthy is extremely important! A week before my SAT I got shingles, which were caused by stress. It was an awful thing to have to go to my junior prom with shingles because I was worried about the SAT. So stay calm!

> —*TERESA*
> *PLANTSVILLE, CONNECTICUT*
> *SAT/ACT SCORES: 1190*
> *UNIVERSITY OF CONNECTICUT*

• • • • • • • •

MAKE CHAUCER YOUR FRIEND. The best way to prepare for the SAT is reading British literature to improve your reading comprehension. I didn't spend time memorizing and I got every reading comprehension question right.

> —*BRIAN WU*
> *CORONA, CALIFORNIA*
> *SAT/ACT SCORES: 2360*
> *UNDECIDED*

• • • • • • • •

ONE THING THAT MY FRIEND and I joked about after all the SAT craziness was how we used to trick ourselves into thinking that we were studying really hard. You know, you buy a million prep books and you carry them around diligently and even though you never crack them open you feel that you are doing something just by having them there. But it's a false sense of security. You really have to study and know that your future is riding on this test, regardless of how much you hate it or how unfair you think it is. Because when it comes down to it, the admissions officers need a way to distinguish you from the million others.

> —*VIDYA SATHYAMOORTHY*
> *ROCKVILLE, MARYLAND*
> *SAT/ACT SCORES: 2160/33*
> *UNDECIDED*

The prep books can get costly, so if you know someone who's finished taking the tests you might want to trade your books. I traded my SAT II books for a friend's SAT I books, which cut down on cost.

> —*QUINCY CHUCK*
> *HONG KONG*
> *SAT/ACT SCORES: 2190*
> *UNDECIDED*

HEADLINES
Best Advice and Top Tips

- Read, read, read! It helps with improving vocabulary as well as reading comprehension.
- Figure out the best way to study *for you*. Classes? Private tutor? Group study? Solo study?
- Map out a study plan of attack, then follow it.

I WAS REALLY INTIMIDATED by the Math section at first. The first time I ever took a real practice test after the PSAT, I think I got nine wrong in one section! I tried not to be discouraged and went back and reviewed why I had gotten each problem wrong. I started to recognize patterns and similar types of questions that the College Board tends to ask. From that point on, the sight of a familiar type of question prevented me from panicking. I also stopped consuming valuable time by refusing to stay stuck on a particular question. I moved on, found one that I could answer with confidence, and then went back to it.

—*STEPHANIE*
NEW FAIRFIELD, CONNECTICUT
SAT/ACT SCORES: 2300
UNDECIDED

• • • • • • • •

PREPARATION IS THE KEY; the decision as to how well you will be prepared for the test is strictly up to you.

—*ANONYMOUS*
NEW YORK, NEW YORK
NEW YORK UNIVERSITY

I STUDIED FOR ABOUT TWO HOURS a week for two months from the College Board book. What worked for me was finishing a practice test, going back and looking at my mistakes. Figure out why you are getting problems wrong. Mark those problems. A month later, go back to it. Make sure you understand it this time.

—*ANONYMOUS*
ORADELL, NEW JERSEY
SAT/ACT SCORES: 2350
UNDECIDED

* * * * * * * *

COMING FROM CANADA, I hadn't had the slightest preparation for the SATs or what they really were. Kaplan helped me with answer strategies, study guides, and they stimulate tests so that we can adapt to other pressures like time and following instructions. It's those types of things (like time management) that most people tend not to focus on or even realize until they actually take their SATs.

—*ELANA JUDITH SYRTASH*
NEW YORK, NEW YORK
YESHIVA UNIVERSITY

* * * * * * * *

I TOOK THE SAT a total of three times and my score increased each time, about 100 points in total. I took an SAT prep course and that certainly helped, but I'd say a lot of it had to do with experience. When I went into my first test, I really didn't know what to expect and was certainly more nervous than I should have been. But after getting one test under my belt I knew what my weak areas were and how to better prepare for the next time.

—*BLAYNE ALEXANDER*
EDMOND, OKLAHOMA
DUKE UNIVERSITY

SMELLS LIKE SAT SPIRIT

Whenever I studied for the SATs I wore the same perfume (Ralph Lauren's Romance) and sucked on the same candy (Lemonheads). When it came time to actually take the test, I again wore Romance and sucked on Lemonheads. Your senses of smell and taste are very strong; they can put you back in the same element so you'll remember better.

—*DANIELLE SILBER*
ST. LOUIS, MISSOURI
WASHINGTON UNIVERSITY IN ST. LOUIS

GET YOURSELF THE PRINCETON REVIEW prep book for your test and work through it cover to cover. Studying one month, maybe two, for an hour a day should guarantee you a good score.

—*B.P.*
EVANSTON, ILLINOIS
SAT/ACT SCORES: 2200/33
NORTHWESTERN UNIVERSITY

AT FIRST I USED FLASH CARDS for vocabulary, but once I started taking practice tests, I realized that the same base of about 400-500 words were used repeatedly. I knew about half of them right off the bat. Just by taking the tests I was able to figure out some of the words I didn't know right away, and I looked up the words that I was really having trouble with and couldn't figure out from the prefixes and suffixes and just common ideas of what the word might be. There were maybe about 20-30 words that I had to study and memorize. There's a definite cycle of words that they use.

—*AARON*
BEVERLY HILLS, CALIFORNIA
SAT/ACT SCORES: 2150
UNIVERSITY OF CALIFORNIA, BERKELEY

THE FIRST TIME I TOOK the SAT I scored 2090, which is very good by most standards, but kind of disappointed me because of the average scores of the schools I was looking at. So I bought the College Board book and started buckling down. A lot of people turn to those review classes, but the book, with all its practice tests, is much more valuable. I tried to do about a 20-minute section a day, and corrected my errors as I went. There are always going to be things you don't understand, but the SAT is simple enough that usually an English or a math teacher offers the best help you can get. I gained 150 points after taking five practice tests. I feel confident I could have done even better with a little more practice.

> —ANONYMOUS
> ILLINOIS
> SAT/ACT SCORES: 2240/35
> YALE UNIVERSITY

I created an SAT schedule for myself to make sure I was studying at a good pace.

—BRITTANY ELYSE GRAHAM
WEST CHESTER, PENNSYLVANIA
SAT/ACT SCORES: 890/21
INDIANA UNIVERSITY OF PENNSYLVANIA

• • • • • • • •

I THINK IT IS MORE BENEFICIAL to take the PSAT and be in the same environment that you will have when you take the SAT, rather than study at home with old practice tests. At home you have distractions. I found that when I studied at home I would frequently stop the clock, check my e-mail, or eat.

> —ANONYMOUS
> LAS VEGAS, NEVADA
> SAT/ACT SCORES: 2300
> VANDERBILT UNIVERSITY

• • • • • • • •

I WISH I'D TAKEN THE WHOLE practice test at one sitting, rather than on different days, so it would be more like the actual experience. Taking it all at once multiple times would have really helped.

> —JIN KIM
> ST. LOUIS, MISSOURI
> SAT/ACT SCORES: 1260/28
> WASHINGTON UNIVERSITY IN ST. LOUIS

Consider

WHEN YOU STUDY VOCABULARY WORDS, don't just look at the definition. Look at the word, get the part of speech, and look at it in a sentence. Define the word from context and then write a sentence that someone else could use to define the word. After that, look up the definition. It's slow and tedious but it really gets you to learn.

—*ANONYMOUS*
SIMI VALLEY, CALIFORNIA
SAT/ACT SCORES: 2230
UNDECIDED

• • • • • • •

" When you take a class, you want to make sure that you have an instructor who is going to crack the whip. "

—*RAYNA*
NEEDHAM, MASSACHUSETTS
SAT/ACT SCORES: 2280
CLAREMONT MCKENNA COLLEGE

• • • • • • • •

I ATTENDED ONE SESSION of a Princeton Review class, but that was way too impersonal. I was much more comfortable with a one-on-one tutor, which ultimately proved to be of great assistance. I went to the English tutor once a week for about three months. I'd recommend personalized tutoring if it fits into your schedule and budget.

—*DREW SILVERMAN*
ELKINS PARK, PENNSYLVANIA
SAT/ACT SCORES: 1410
SYRACUSE UNIVERSITY

THE WAY TO WORD POWER

The best way to train for the SAT Reading sections involves no studying at all: Just read. Read as much as possible. If you read just a few articles in *The New York Times* every day for a year, you will have encountered a huge percentage of the words you'll encounter in the SAT. The test won't even seem like a test anymore. Other tips for vocabulary:

- While you're reading, watching TV, etc., carry around a notebook with you. List all the words you don't know. Look them up when you get home. This is the best way to really learn new words. There's no way you're going to learn every word in the English language, nor do you need to.
- Concentrate on the words the SAT uses the most, which can be found on Sparknotes.com, in The Princeton Review's guidebooks, and elsewhere.

—*Timothy Michael Cooper*
New York, New York
Yale University

MOST GOOD READERS CAN KNOW approximately what a word means just by reading it over and over in books. Also, knowing vocabulary serves a greater purpose. When you get to college, you will obviously need at least a mildly broad vocabulary, and many people fail to realize this. I regularly do the SAT Question of the Day, and I find that the vocabulary questions are pretty useful. They explain the correct word, and sometimes words that are completely off, so you start to learn words gradually.

—*John*
Venice, California
SAT/ACT Scores: 2290
Undecided

I recommend SAT flash cards. They are a stress-free way to study and you can use them alone or with a partner.

—*BLAYNE ALEXANDER*
EDMOND,
OKLAHOMA
DUKE
UNIVERSITY

DON'T THINK THAT JUST BECAUSE you're taking lots of advanced placement classes in an academic school that these will prepare you for the SAT; they won't. The only thing that will specifically prepare you is a review class. And although a review class may be expensive, it's worth it. I took a review class and did tons of practice tests to help prepare. I'm convinced that all those practice tests helped me do better.

—*MICHAL ROSENOER*
CORTE MADERA, CALIFORNIA
SAT/ACT SCORES: 2220
UNIVERSITY OF CALIFORNIA, BERKELEY

• • • • • • • •

I IDENTIFIED MY WEAKNESSES and realized that if I was ever going to master the sentence completion section I needed to greatly enhance my vocabulary. Rather than attacking those generic SAT word lists, I actually began to write down unknown words while I was reading. I'd have a decent-sized list when I was done and I would go back and look them up. It was tedious at first but I started to see a lot of repetition and familiarity. I remember reading *Jane Eyre, The Awakening,* and *Absalom, Absalom.* It helped me greatly. I recently found one of my old word lists and found that I knew all of them.

—*STEPHANIE*
NEW FAIRFIELD, CONNECTICUT
SAT/ACT SCORES: 2300
UNDECIDED

• • • • • • • •

LEARNING THE VOCABULARY THROUGH a study guide helped me go faster on the test. Because I was so familiar with those words, I didn't have to spend time figuring out what they meant by using context.

—*ALEX*
BIRMINGHAM, ALABAMA
SAT/ACT SCORES: 2350/36

I TOOK A CLASS CALLED REVOLUTION PREP and I had to take one SAT practice test every Saturday morning for 12 weeks. After I took the course my scores went up a few hundred points, so I am convinced that the best way to practice is to take practice tests all the time.

—*LINDSAY*
LOS ANGELES, CALIFORNIA
SAT/ACT SCORES: 1760
UNIVERSITY OF CALIFORNIA, SANTA BARBARA

" I studied with my friends for the Math part of the SAT. Some of us were better at certain problems, like Algebra II, and others were better at logic word problems. We all gained from each other's expertise. "

—*MOLLY*
LAS VEGAS, NEVADA
UNIVERSITY OF ARIZONA

I FOLLOWED THE ADVICE of an upperclassman friend of mine and signed up to have the College Board e-mail me The Official SAT Question of the Day. You can sign up on their Web site. I did one of those practice questions every day for about three months prior to taking the test, and that really helped me feel prepared.

—*CAITLIN MYERS*
CINCINNATI, OHIO
SAT/ACT SCORES: 1929/29
MIAMI UNIVERSITY

Consider

Taking the test is the best preparation you can have for taking the test.

—*ANONYMOUS*
ST. LOUIS,
MISSOURI
WILLIAMS COLLEGE

I WOULD NOT STUDY WITH FRIENDS because it is too distracting. I invited some girlfriends over to study one time and we ended up playing drinking games all night. That was the last time I studied with a group. Not only didn't I accomplish anything that night, but the next day I was so hung over that I missed studying that day too.

—*ASHLEY*
SAN FRANCISCO, CALIFORNIA
SAT/ACT SCORES: 2100
UNIVERSITY OF SOUTHERN CALIFORNIA

• • • • • • • •

I SIGNED UP FOR AN SAT STUDY course outside of my school because everyone else I knew was taking it. I only went for a few days and then I dropped it. I thought that it was expensive and I didn't think it was worth the money. All they did was give us work and force us to do it, so I figured I could just get a book and force myself to do it on my own.

—*DILCIA LOOMIS*
BUENA PARK, CALIFORNIA
CLAREMONT MCKENNA COLLEGE

• • • • • • • •

PRIVATE TUTORING WORKED BEST FOR ME. I took the Princeton Review class in the fall. Then I began self-studying around the first week in December for the January SAT, and I met with a tutor once a week to go over practice problems. Classes like the one I took are easy to lose concentration in and you can be easily distracted, especially with friends in the class. Private tutors force you to practice on your own, and you need to have stuff completed to go over with them.

—*TOM O'BRIEN*
SCRANTON, PENNSYLVANIA
SAT/ACT SCORES: 2160
UNDECIDED

SUMMER SCHOOL?

If you are going to take an SAT preparation class, take it in the summer. There are a couple of reasons to take a summer course rather than a class during the year. The class that I took over the summer was five nights a week for three weeks. During the school year, I think it's about one night a week for a longer period of time. So the summer class is more intense. It's also better to take it over the summer because once school starts, studying for the SAT can get pretty overwhelming. I had so much going on once school started and I know I would have never made the class, even once a week.

—Louis S. Wu
Silver Spring, Maryland
SAT/ACT Scores: 2300
University of Maryland

THE VERBAL PART OF THE SAT was challenging for me. I found dictionary.com helpful. I signed up for their word-of-the-day e-mail where they send you a new word and definition daily. This really increased my vocabulary and prepared me for the test.

—Kira
Fresno, California
SAT/ACT Scores: 1340

I WORKED FOR AN SAT prep course in exchange for private tutoring lessons. They really helped with my scores, so if you don't have the money, I would definitely approach a local test preparation center and see if they are up to some kind of bartering.

—Lindsay
Los Angeles, California
SAT/ACT Scores: 1760
University of California, Santa Barbara

You will get so sick of taking tests, but I guarantee that nothing will surprise you on the day of the actual exam.

—SARAH CARRIER
  NORTH GRANBY,
  CONNECTICUT
  WASHINGTON
  UNIVERSITY IN ST.
  LOUIS

TO PREPARE FOR THE SAT I took a class over the summer before my junior year. The class lasted for two months and met for three hours, three times a week. The class really helped because I scored 2100 on my first practice SAT test, and when it was time to take the real one I ended up getting 2360.

—PATTY LU
  TINTON FALLS, NEW JERSEY
  SAT/ACT SCORES: 2360
  UNDECIDED

• • • • • • • •

IN HIGH SCHOOL, I dropped out of Algebra II. I tried so hard, but I just couldn't get it. I convinced my school to let me drop out of math and instead just have a math tutor outside of school. My tutor happened to be trained in SAT preparation, so I got her to help me prepare for the SAT instead of for high school math. In the end, I got her to give me a great grade in the "class" and at the same time got the services of a private tutor for the SAT, twice a week.

—EMMA
  WASHINGTON, D.C.
  SAT/ACT SCORES: 1890
  PITZER COLLEGE

• • • • • • • •

I RECOMMEND STARTING ABOUT four to six months before. What worked best for me was taking the old tests; but don't always do them all the way through. Sometimes I would take a complete test, but most of the time I would just do one section. You want to get a sense of what it will be like in the testing center, but at the same time you don't want to put too much pressure on yourself.

—AMAR PANJWANI
  APPLE VALLEY, CALIFORNIA
  UNDECIDED

CYBER-STUDYING

Ifound an SAT prep site that helped me out called acethesat.com. It was good because it was the only site that gave actual step-by-step processes for answering questions. Although its product is basically a PDF file, it really helps because it is concise and not condescending like other books. I used that, and the College Board book because it is the only source of real SATs.

The only thing that these sources did not help me with was advanced math skills, which I found help on mostly through another site, satmathpro.com. It was useful because it helped with advanced math problems through video teaching. I also got a little bit of extra help on infamous "rate" problems through collegeconfidential.com message boards. It's easy to sign up and create an account. Then you just create a topic asking a question about the SAT, and someone else out there in cyberspace will answer it.

—*Matthew Haber*
Holland, Pennsylvania
SAT/ACT Scores: 2300
Cornell University

I STUDIED FOR THE SAT on my own and in a group. When you learn one-on-one, there are the advantages to the individual attention you get. But there is something about learning in a group that works for me. You're all in the same boat and you can work together to learn.

—*Brandon Malki*
West Orange, New Jersey
SAT/ACT Scores: 1300
Bloomsburg University of Pennsylvania

Consider

My 10TH-grade English teacher was the most helpful person in preparing for the Verbal section. Using the book *1100 Words You Need to Know*, we had comprehensive vocabulary exams throughout the year that resulted in the entire class learning 1,100 common SAT words. I suggest that everyone take at least a class (or study profusely on your own) that solely builds vocabulary. My mother also arranged private verbal and math tutors that came to my home once a week for the few months leading up to the exam.

> —BETH LORI WECKSELL
> GREAT NECK, NEW YORK
> SAT/ACT SCORES: 1370
> TUFTS UNIVERSITY

• • • • • • • •

Take the practice tests. I found that my Math score went up without me really doing anything from junior to senior year. You just have to practice. The more you answer those types of questions the more comfortable you will be when you actually take the test. There are no "new" questions, so the more familiar you are with samples, the better it will be.

> —MERYL BRANCH-MCTIERNAN
> BROOKLYN, NEW YORK
> SAT/ACT SCORES: 1360
> SYRACUSE UNIVERSITY

• • • • • • • •

Take the College Board's "Blue Book," the one with a ton of released SATs. It's all about getting a good feel for the patterns. You can pick up tricks here and there, but nothing replaces solid practice.

> —ANONYMOUS
> WASHINGTON, D.C.
> SAT/ACT SCORES: 2300
> DARTMOUTH COLLEGE

I **IMPROVED MY PSAT** score by: 1) using Renee Mazer's vocabulary tapes *(Not Too Scary Vocabulary)*. They're hilarious. They include songs and funny scenarios, and they helped a lot; 2) learning a few grammar/style rules, like what parallelism is and such. Any test-prep book will help with that; 3) my dad paid this high school junior to study with me (he called it "babysitting"). We went over a lot of practice tests together, which probably helped. The improvement from 8th to 10th grade (1470 to 2390) came pretty naturally; since I got more practice reading and writing, I naturally became a slightly better reader and writer.

> —JESSICA
> BOCA RATON, FLORIDA
> SAT/ACT SCORES: 2390
> CALIFORNIA INSTITUTE OF TECHNOLOGY

● ● ● ● ● ● ● ●

I **REALLY WANTED TO TAKE** the SAT courses but there was no way my family could pay for that. So I went to the Princeton and Kaplan centers and bought their curriculum/lesson plan books. I also purchased numerous SAT books, including the one provided by the College Board. And whenever I had time, I solved problems and took test after test. Of course, I had school, friends, and, you know, life, so I did all this mostly late at night or during breaks. It was all worth it when my scores went up over 400 points.

> —JIKYU CHOI
> FAIR OAKS, CALIFORNIA
> SAT/ACT SCORES: 2370
> STANFORD UNIVERSITY

Don't study with anyone else. Since you are going to be taking the test alone, you should study by yourself, too.

> —MICHAEL WYMBS
> BEACH HAVEN,
> NEW JERSEY
> SAT/ACT
> SCORES: 2260

"Those who do not study are only cattle dressed up in men's clothes."

—CHINESE PROVERB

SERIOUSLY!

Go buy a practice test compilation. Don't borrow it from the library or pay for it, skim over it, then return it to the bookstore and get $20 back. Buy it! This is so that you can mark, scrawl and notate all over it without reservation. (Or, if you'd like, stab it repeatedly with a pencil in frustration.)

Then take the test, just as you would when you're taking the real test. Lock the door, close the window, shut down the computer, turn off the stereo, put away the iPod and snacks, clear the desk, and kick the cat and/or dog and/or younger sibling out of the room. There should only be you, the test, writing utensils and a clock to keep the time. And do keep the time, especially if you find yourself running out of it frequently.

You need to learn how to work quickly and accurately. Do write the essay, before you start on everything else, just like in the real test. Afterward, ask someone else to grade it for you, unless you think you can be honest to yourself.

    —JAWON LEE
    SAN DIEGO, CALIFORNIA
    SAT/ACT SCORES: 2400

I BOUGHT A BOOK AND STUDIED on my own. I started preparing about two months before the exam by taking practice tests and going over the results. Every weekend, sometimes one day, and sometimes two, I would pick a section and complete it. I never sat down for four hours to take an entire exam, and sometimes I blew off a weekend, but that's okay. My friends spent thousands of dollars on tutors, and most of them hardly saw an increase in scores. A lot of people think the classes and tutoring help, but those people have no desire to do well, they just want a free ticket to a good score. As long as you want to do well and want to study, you can just do it on your own.

> —*NIKITA BIER*
> *PALOS VERDES, CALIFORNIA*
> *SAT/ACT SCORES: 2100*
> *STANFORD UNIVERSITY*

. . . .

I LIKED PRINCETON REVIEW'S *Word Smart* book for vocabulary. Just read it whenever or wherever you are. Read it when you are a passenger in a car, at the dinner table; just read it repeatedly. It's much easier to incorporate the reading into your daily activities.

> —*JOHN*
> *AUSTIN, TEXAS*
> *SAT/ACT SCORES: 2100*
> *BOSTON UNIVERSITY*

. . . .

THE FIRST TWO TIMES I took the test I did the Princeton Review class, and I don't think it helped me. I got the same score twice. But then my parents got me a private tutor and my score went up over a hundred points. I got way more out of the one-on-one attention.

> —*STEFANIE LAMPRECHT*
> *TIBURON, CALIFORNIA*
> *SAT/ACT SCORES: 1800*
> *SANTA CLARA UNIVERSITY*

THE THIRD TIME I TOOK IT all I did was just buy one of those Kaplan books. I had friends who spent over $1,000 on a tutor, but if you're willing to do the work you can get just as much out of a $15 book.

—*ANDREW TIMBERLAKE*
BIRMINGHAM, ALABAMA
SAT/ACT SCORES: 2400
YALE UNIVERSITY

· · · · · · · · ·

"The best thing that I ever did to prepare for the SAT was to buy an SAT practice CD. I spent at least an hour a day studying and taking practice tests with the CD and it raised my score substantially."

—*BRITTANY MCCOMBS*
VENICE, CALIFORNIA
SAT/ACT SCORES: 1000
SYRACUSE UNIVERSITY

· · · · · · · · ·

STUDY ON YOUR OWN. Get a book, learn test-taking strategies, and start incorporating new vocabulary words into your daily routine. I took all of the classes available to me and I do not think they helped.

—*PAIGE HILL*
MONTEREY, CALIFORNIA
UNIVERSITY OF CALIFORNIA, LOS ANGELES

WHEN PREPARING FOR THE TEST, be more attentive to vocabulary words that may crop up in conversation, on television, in movies, and of course in print. There were several words on the SAT I was sure I had never heard before, but after taking the test, I started noticing them being used by other people in conversation and in my textbooks.

—*CLAIRE*
EL PASO, TEXAS
SAT/ACT SCORES: 2280/33
CLEMSON UNIVERSITY

* * * * * * * *

START WITH A PRACTICE TEST and compare your score to the average scores for the colleges that you want to apply for, and then you can tailor your studying to how much you need to improve. So if you felt totally overwhelmed on the practice test, you should probably take a course, but if you feel that you are almost where you want to be, you can use a book to review the specific areas that you need to work on.

—*BEN*
SPRINGFIELD, ILLINOIS
SAT/ACT SCORES: 2200/32
UNIVERSITY OF ILLINOIS, URBANA-CHAMPAIGN

* * * * * * * *

I DIDN'T ENROLL FOR AN SAT prep course for a couple of reasons. First, I worked five nights a week and I didn't want to have something else to do when I had a night off. Second, they are pretty expensive. So I figured I would just take them and see how I'd do. You always hear that the test just tests your natural ability. I took it twice and wound up with a score that was basically where I expected to be.

—*ERIC GOULD*
CHESHIRE, CONNECTICUT
SAT/ACT SCORES: 1050
HOFSTRA UNIVERSITY

I highly recommend getting a tutor. Success on the SAT is based on learning the different rules that the College Board tries to trick you with!

—*Marin Hawk*
Ridgefield,
Connecticut
SAT/ACT Scores:
2260/33
Washington University in St. Louis

If you take a prep class and then take the test multiple times, it's important to review the material they taught you in that class between tests. I took a class for the SAT through my school, and then took the test at the end of that class, in the spring of my junior year. After the class, I did very well. But when I took the SAT again in the fall of my senior year, my score went down 110 points because I didn't review.

—*Teresa*
Plantsville, Connecticut
SAT/ACT Scores: 1190
University of Connecticut

• • • • • • • •

I don't believe in memorizing vocabulary at all. There's no point—you either have the knowledge to begin with, or you don't. It takes years of reading to develop a full vocabulary. You can't cram. It's better to do some questions and learn the question style. Most of the time you don't need to understand all, or even most of it. You just need to be able to get a general idea of what's going on. I got an 800 in Critical Reading and there were definitely two or three words in there I wasn't sure about.

—*Anonymous*
Miami, Florida
SAT/ACT Scores: 2320
Columbia University

• • • • • • • •

I was happy with my scores and happy with the amount of time I studied. I could have studied more and could have done a lot better, but I didn't think it was worth the time I would have had to commit. I don't think you can change your scores that much once you already do well.

—*Dilcia Loomis*
Buena Park, California
Claremont McKenna College

SEE A PATTERN HERE?

Get to know the test well. Studying the "Blue Book" and other study guides actually does help. Patterns start to emerge in each section, making the big test day much more predictable. There really are no catches. For the Critical Reading section especially, I began to notice patterns. The basic layout of the test was always the same, with the small passages, comparative passages and long passages all coming in the same order. This made the test day a much more predictable event. Also, I was able to notice more subtle patterns within the questions and passages themselves. The questions would always be, at the most basic level, the same in each test. There would always be a "context clue definition" question, a "theme" question, a "similarity" question as well as other basic questions which repeated themselves in one form or another in each test I had taken.

—*Kevin Wandrei*
Adams, Massachusetts
SAT/ACT Scores: 1260/28
University of Southern California

SOME PEOPLE THINK IT'S DUMB to take SAT prep classes because the SAT is just supposed to test your aptitude. True, but how would you feel if a dumb friend of yours somehow got into Duke while you're stuck at a community college, all because you were unfamiliar with the structure of the exam and the types of questions they provide, thereby resulting in a low SAT score? Think of prep classes as an investment to make your profile that much more appealing.

—*Solomon Chang*
Providence, Rhode Island
SAT/ACT Scores: 1410
College of William and Mary

I TOOK THE PSAT FIRST to see where I was in math. Since I didn't do that well, my parents hired a private tutor, but just for math. Before I had my tutor, I would just look at the first few words of a problem, not understand the problem and either skip it or guess it. The tutor taught me how to read them and understand them and decipher what they were asking.

—*JOCELYN*
   BEVERLY HILLS, CALIFORNIA
   SAT/ACT SCORES: 1540
   UNIVERSITY OF ARIZONA

• • • • • • • •

I DON'T BELIEVE ANY CLASS OUTSIDE of school is an effective use of one's time. The SAT is not something that can easily be taught to a student. It's designed to test how much you've learned in all of your schooling, so you can't make that time up in a few hours a week. Also, many of my friends were so sick of looking at SAT problems due to these classes that they ended up doing worse on the test.

—*PHILLIP LAVIN*
   MARIETTA, GEORGIA

• • • • • • • •

VIEW DISCOURAGING PSAT subsection scores as springboards rather than vexations. My advice for math is pretty generic (unfortunately): note the question types that present the greatest problems for you and practice them. Since I have trouble completing an entire practice test, I focused on the "hard" problems and skipped the ones classified as easy (the ones I knew I could get right). I'd usually do the last 10 problems of each Math section and found that this conserved time while allowing me to focus on the true problem areas.

—*STEPHANIE*
   NEW FAIRFIELD, CONNECTICUT
   SAT/ACT SCORES: 2300
   UNDECIDED

THE FORMULA REALLY DOES come down to stretching one's mind from a young age with things like math team and reading *The New York Times* every day. I could take an intellectually average (but willing!) 6th grader, and after five years of math enrichment, essay work, and bookworming (hopefully with a love of reading instilled since age 5 or so), and have them turn out at least a 2000 combined score. Does that mean the trick is 50 percent parenting, 30 percent good teachers, and 20 percent plain mental horsepower? Yeah, that sounds about right.

> —*STEVE ESTES*
> *NEW YORK, NEW YORK*
> *SAT/ACT SCORES: 2380*
> *COLUMBIA UNIVERSITY*

No shortage of study material: A search for "SAT Test" on Amazon's Books section netted over 7,500 results.

• • • • • • • • •

THE BEST WAY TO SCORE WELL on the ACTs is to have a well-rounded education inside and outside of school. For as long as I could remember, my mom was always taking my sister and me to anything educational she could get her hands on. We had videos on evolution, the solar system, Native Americans, and more. When I took the ACTs, most of the questions were easy because I was familiar with the content. After taking two practice tests, I knew I wouldn't have a problem getting at least a 26. It would seem very hard to cram years of education into a four-week study session, which so many of my classmates did and still didn't score above a 22.

> —*ZAKIA SIPP*
> *CHICAGO, ILLINOIS*
> *SAT/ACT SCORES: 28*
> *CHICAGO STATE UNIVERSITY*

FINDING A GOOD SAT CLASS OR TUTOR

CONSIDER YOUR LEARNING STYLE. Are you comfortable learning in a large group setting, where you can take notes and absorb strategies but not interact much with the instructor? Do you do better studying in small groups? Would you prefer to work one-on-one with a private tutor?

DO YOUR RESEARCH. There's no advanced degree or certification required to be an SAT instructor. That's why instructors run the gamut, from established professionals who aced the SAT to jokers without any real SAT knowledge. So before you choose a teacher or tutor, find out a little background, including years of experience and what he or she scored on the actual exam. Also, don't assume that a big company will have the best people—the biggest firms often pay their instructors the least and hire people who look and sound good but may not have done as well on the SAT.

FIND AN OPTION THAT FITS YOUR ABILITY LEVEL. Classes usually work best when everyone is at *roughly* the same level. If you're way ahead of or behind the rest of the pack, you may want to consider a course designed for someone at your level or hire a private one-on-one tutor.

JUST READ A LOT. It doesn't matter what you read, just as long as you do it. You should bookmark *The New York Times* and *The Los Angeles Times*. I pick up a lot of words from blogs I read, and those are things I enjoy reading. Just look up every word you don't know and make a list of all the words you collect.

> —*JOHN*
> *AUSTIN, TEXAS*
> *SAT/ACT SCORES: 2100*
> *BOSTON UNIVERSITY*

. . . .

I WENT THROUGH AS MANY ACT practice books as possible. I started studying in February for my first attempt at the test. From then until September, I probably went through about 10-15 books, taking about 20-30 practice tests in all. Even two weeks before the September test, I had my mom get me two more books. I really started the intense studying for the September test in July, since I knew that it would be the last time I would be able to take it if I wanted to apply to a school early decision.

> —*LAUREN*
> *POTOMAC, MARYLAND*
> *SAT/ACT SCORES: 33*
> *CORNELL UNIVERSITY*

. . . .

PRACTICE MAKES PERFECT. Challenge yourself and your friends by reviewing math basics so that you can use them later on. You can't expect to do well on the tougher questions if your 1-2-3's are too slow or rusty. Also, for vocabulary words, always look at the root. Even if you don't know the meaning, there are almost always similarities to other words you know, within their base, to help you figure them out!

> —*ELANA JUDITH SYRTASH*
> *NEW YORK, NEW YORK*
> *YESHIVA UNIVERSITY*

I USUALLY PRACTICED WITH the official College Board SAT study guide, and did so by reading the test-taking strategies first. I think that actual practice is the most important part of preparation—it does more for you than any class can if you can identify your errors. Instead of doing whole sections, I timed myself on individual sections (then redid them to make sure I could remember how to do them right). It was frustrating at first, but I noticed a steady improvement.

—JOSEPH ANDA
LITTLE ROCK, ARKANSAS
SAT/ACT SCORES: 2300
UNDECIDED

❝My parents really wanted me to take an SAT practice course. I was so mad at them for making me go early on Saturdays. Now, I have no doubt that the practice helped me get a score that made me proud, got me a great scholarship, and prompted my parents to buy me a new car!❞

—JOSH SCOTT FEINSTEIN
MASSAPEQUA PARK, NEW YORK
SAT/ACT SCORES: 1470
WASHINGTON UNIVERSITY IN ST. LOUIS

OTHER SAT STUDY OPTIONS

STUDY WITH FRIENDS. A study group can be a fun (and free!) way to make sure you're devoting time to the SAT. Having a group of friends nearby can make SAT prep easier to deal with and you can help each other with tough problems. Just make sure to stay focused!

GO ONLINE. The Internet is full of SAT study options. While the big companies offer expensive online courses (not always a great choice), there's also lots of free help. The College Board offers free practice questions and even a free sample practice test at http://www.collegeboard.com/student/testing/sat/prep_one/ prep_one.html.

STUDY ALONE. If you've got the discipline and can set aside the time, simply studying on your own with prep books can be a perfectly good option. You can either buy practice books from the top test prep firms or simply use the College Board's *Official SAT Study Guide*.

AFTER YOU TAKE A PRACTICE TEST, go over every answer, including the ones you got right. Spend time on every answer until you understand exactly why the College Board claims it's better than the other four answer choices. Just checking your score is not good enough and will not get you higher scores.

—*MICHAEL WYMBS*
BEACH HAVEN, NEW JERSEY
SAT/ACT SCORES: 2260

Learn to use your time well, and you're already halfway to a high score.

—*JAWON LEE*
SAN DIEGO, CALIFORNIA
SAT/ACT SCORES: 2400

IF YOU WANT TO IMPROVE your scores on the Math section, study and memorize formulas. There are generic algebra and geometry formulas that you can find online and in study guides. Memorize them because you can apply them to a lot of problems that appear on the test.

—*BRADLEY HOUSTON*
AUSTIN, TEXAS
SAT/ACT SCORES: 2050/32
RICE UNIVERSITY

I FOUND THE PRINCETON REVIEW book to be the most useful because it made use of tests which seemed more difficult than the actual SAT, while still providing a format similar to that of the SAT. After my first exam, I studied the Math section rigorously, simply by doing practice tests and examples over and over again. My score in Math improved 110 points. The second time around, I did the same with Critical Reading, but I also used Kaplan's vocabulary words, and studied the flash cards about a half hour each day. My score only improved 30 points this time, which may have been due to the lesser amount of time I had to study in between exam dates.

—*KEVIN WANDREI*
ADAMS, MASSACHUSETTS
SAT/ACT SCORES: 1260/28
UNIVERSITY OF SOUTHERN CALIFORNIA

I AM MUCH BETTER AT MATH THAN ENGLISH, so I really focused on the Math section when I studied. I think the effort you have to put in to increase your scores in a certain section is not worth the payoff. I knew that I would just be wasting time. Realistically, my scores might have improved about 50 points on the Reading Comprehension, and to attain that I would have had to spend several weekends practicing. Make your effort on the stuff you know you can improve.

—CODY
PHOENIX, ARIZONA
SAT/ACT SCORES: 1900
UNIVERSITY OF ARIZONA

I WRESTLED IN HIGH SCHOOL, so it was really hard to balance school, sports and studying for the SAT. Wrestling is one of the most time-consuming sports because the season lasts longer than those of other sports. I mostly tried to get my work done during lunch and when I got home. I didn't always get it all done, but I still got into the college of my choice.

—BURTON DEWITT
MELVILLE, NEW YORK
SAT/ACT SCORES: 2080/32
RICE UNIVERSITY

TRY TO GET YOUR STUDYING DONE on your own schedule when you have the free time, because that way you'll be able to really concentrate on what you're doing. If your parents have to force you to study when they think you need to, you won't be able to focus because you'll be mad about the party or the game or some other fun you're missing out on.

—JOHN STEPHEN REBER
CINCINNATI, OHIO
SAT/ACT SCORES: 2200
GEORGETOWN UNIVERSITY

GOOD SAT STUDY HABITS

START EARLY. Studying properly will require at least dozens of hours of preparation. While cramming may have worked for you in the past, it won't work here. At the latest, you should begin studying during the spring of your junior year.

PLAN YOUR STUDYING. When you first start preparing for the SAT, map out a plan of attack. Figure out what you need to learn and practice, and understand which materials you're going to work through for each section.

STUDY IN A CONSISTENT TIME AND PLACE. You'll be more relaxed and efficient if you set aside a consistent time and place to study, whether it's your bedroom on Tuesday nights or 3rd period study hall.

WORK FOR AT LEAST AN HOUR AT A TIME. The SAT is an ordeal that takes more than four hours to get through. Patience and improving your attention span are key skills. Studying for 15 minutes at a time may help you review concepts, but it won't help your brain get in shape for the actual SAT testing environment.

TIME YOURSELF. The SAT is what's known as a "speeded" test— time is definitely a factor. If you haven't been practicing doing questions with a clock or timer, then you're not ready for the test.

First, I started with basic vocabulary, high-school level; then I moved on to *Word Smart* by Princeton Review. After memorizing those words, I raised my score about 100 points. Then, I started reading magazines, newspapers and books: *The New York Times*, *The Economist* and *U.S. News & World Report*. My score improved every year.

> —*Joon Nam*
> *Murrieta, California*
> *SAT/ACT Scores: 2220*
> *UNDECIDED*

"I didn't spend the week before the test cramming SAT words into my head. Instead, throughout high school, if I didn't know a word I would look it up. "

> —*Anonymous*
> *Seattle, Washington*
> *SAT/ACT Scores: 2320*

The best thing that I did for preparation for the SAT besides tutoring was taking the practice test provided in the free College Board information booklet and full tests provided in the College Board SAT books. Many of the questions on the actual test are extremely similar. I also hired a tutor who helped in terms of learning the styles of questions the SAT asks and logic skills the test is looking for.

> —*Terrahney Wilson*
> *Lithonia, Georgia*
> *SAT/ACT Scores: 1950*
> *UNDECIDED*

DON'T STUDY FOR VERBAL, MATH, and Writing. Just pick one at a time. Chances are that you will get to take the test more than once. I took it five times, and though that is extreme, it only helped my scores. Most people don't take much time to study for the SAT when they have other things going on in high school. I figured out that if I just tried to improve one section of my exam each time and I actually did it, then it was worth what little time I spent studying.

—*RONALD JORDAN HINSON*
LENOIR, NORTH CAROLINA
SAT/ACT SCORES: 1940
CLEMSON UNIVERSITY

Friends, Family & Your School: Do They Help?

*D*ealing with the demands of friends and family can be one of the most stressful aspects of preparing for the SAT. Friends can be a means of social support, and can provide a welcome release valve when the pressures of college admissions become overwhelming. They can also help guide you through the SAT process: helping you study, reminding you when to sign up for the test, and providing important moral support.

But your friends can also make the SAT more difficult. They may have different priorities than you do in the college admissions process. They may not consider a high SAT score, and the diligent studying such a high score requires, as important as you do—or even as important as a trip to a party, the mall, or the beach. On the other hand, your friends might talk incessantly about the SAT, stressing you out and making it impossible for you to get your mind off the test and relax.

Your parents, meanwhile, can similarly be both a blessing and a burden. They'll support you emotionally, pay for tutors or prep books, and nag you to keep studying and keep the SAT a top priority (you'll thank them later). But parents can also be a major stressor, as they inevitably worry about how you're doing and whether you're preparing enough.

And where does your school fit into all this—guidance counselors, teachers and other mentors who might be able to help you? What should you expect from your school?

Here's some advice about managing your relationships while you study for and take the SAT.

MY MOTHER AND FATHER actually threw me a surprise ACT party two days before the exam. It was just my parents, sister, grandmother, my two favorite cousins, and my best friend. They all cheered me on and said I would do well. My dad kept giving me random ACT questions. And there was a big chocolate cake that said, "A Perfect 36, Ace the ACT." It was nice, but weird. When I saw the cake, I started to feel a little pressure to score a perfect. But scoring a perfect was like winning the lottery. I didn't want to disappoint my father. However, on the day of the test, he reassured me that he believes in me, and whatever score I got would be perfect.

> —ZAKIA SIPP
> CHICAGO, ILLINOIS
> SAT/ACT SCORES: 28
> CHICAGO STATE UNIVERSITY

Some people's parents can intimidate them, which might cause more stress on the child and cause them to not do as well on the SAT.

> —BRITTANY ELYSE GRAHAM
> WEST CHESTER, PENNSYLVANIA
> SAT/ACT SCORES: 890/21
> INDIANA UNIVERSITY OF PENNSYLVANIA

MY PARENTS BOUGHT STUDY books and gave me encouragement, something that I found extremely helpful. They told me that they had faith that I was going to do well. After the results came, they told me my score was excellent. Yes, having supportive parents is, I feel, key to doing well in anything such as this.

> —ASHRAF EASSA
> WINDAM, NEW HAMPSHIRE
> SAT/ACT SCORES: 2040
> MASSACHUSETTS INSTITUTE OF TECHNOLOGY

PAIR OF ACES

In the summer of 2006, Jakub Voboril, a 17-year-old from Kansas, aced both the ACT and the SAT. It's not known how many students have accomplished the feat, but a College Board spokesman admitted, "It's a very, very small number."

HEAD**LINES**
Best Advice and Top Tips

- Regular communication with your parents on your SAT studies will help reduce stress—for them, and for you!
- Only study with friends if you are certain they can be as serious about the test as you are.

MY PARENTS WERE EXTREMELY helpful in motivating me to study. Without them, I do not think I would have been able to sit down and really focus. My parents didn't say anything negative during the entire process. Also, as harsh as it may seem, they virtually forced me to sit down and study during winter break, but I'm ecstatic they did that. There wasn't any grounding or punishments involved. Even though they only "casually" forced me to study, I ultimately glued myself to my chair because, deep inside, I wanted a great score too.

—NEIL SHAH
ENCINO, CALIFORNIA
SAT/ACT SCORES: 2230
UNDECIDED

• • • • • • • •

I ACTUALLY WISH that my parents had pushed me to study.

—BEN
SPRINGFIELD, ILLINOIS
SAT/ACT SCORES: 2200/32
UNIVERSITY OF ILLINOIS, URBANA-CHAMPAIGN

IT IS REALLY HELPFUL TO STUDY with your friends. I had a little study session with my girlfriend and one of my friends before the SAT. All three of us got together and we did a section at a time. Then, after a 25-minute math test, we compared our answers, and if one person got it right and the other wrong then the correct person would teach the wrong one how to do the problem. We got together two times: the Saturday and Wednesday before the test.

—TIM
PHOENIX, ARIZONA
SAT/ACT SCORES: 2130
UNDECIDED

• • • • • • • •

I TRY TO EXPLAIN TO MY PARENTS that scores aren't everything; people with perfect scores get turned down if they're lacking in other areas. They're constantly pressuring me to quit my extracurricular activities and job to focus more on the academics and testing. There's really no easy way to cope with them, so I just try to ignore them.

—YUEYUE GUO
CUMBERLAND, RHODE ISLAND
SAT/ACT SCORES: 2220
UNDECIDED

• • • • • • • •

IT CAN BE HELPFUL to prepare for and take the test at the same time as your friends. When my friends and I found out that we were going to be testing on the same day, I would keep in mind that the others were studying, so I probably should too. And we all had to wake up early on Saturday morning, so staying out late with them was not likely to happen.

—RONALD JORDAN HINSON
LENOIR, NORTH CAROLINA
SAT/ACT SCORES: 1940
CLEMSON UNIVERSITY

YOU WILL DO WELL ON THIS TEST ... OR ELSE!

LIKE ALL CHINESE PARENTS, my parents just nagged all day long for me to study. However, when it came to actually helping me and offering advice on how to take the test, they were little to no help. They have a very skewed view of the college admissions process. So they always said "you're never going to get into Yale, you'll be lucky if you get into University of Rhode Island! You'll never amount to anything in your life! Do you just expect good scores to come from nowhere? No! You have to work hard to get them!" And maybe the nagging helped, just for me to say, "Now I proved you wrong!"

—*YUEYUE GUO*
CUMBERLAND, RHODE ISLAND
SAT/ACT SCORES: 2220
UNDECIDED

· · · · · · · · ·

BACK WHEN I WAS A JUNIOR, when I wanted to go out and spend time with my friends on weekends, my mom would tell me to stay home and read books, memorize vocabulary words and study for SAT. I was already doing this through the weekdays, so I was kind of mad because my parents didn't allow me time to relax. When I look back on it, I look at it as a privilege rather than an annoyance because they just wanted me to succeed in the future. It was just one year of really intense studying and I think it was worth it, especially with the score that I got. And now that I am done with my SAT and all my applications, I am free.

—*JOON NAM*
MURRIETA, CALIFORNIA
SAT/ACT SCORES: 2220
UNDECIDED

IN THE BEGINNING OF MY JUNIOR YEAR of high school, my parents heard about how a lot of other parents put their kids through prep classes to help them get an edge on the whole standardized testing thing. Well, they wouldn't stand the notion of other kids getting high scores because of taking a class geared specifically for the test, so they signed me up for a Princeton Review course. In my opinion, the biggest reason they were pushing for these classes was because I probably didn't seem like I cared enough to study on my own. To be honest, I probably didn't, since it was still early in my second half of high school. I feel kind of bad sometimes because I don't think the prep classes were all that necessary. In that year between the time I took the SAT the first time with the Princeton Review class, and the second time when I studied on my own, I raised my score almost 200 points. So without prep classes, I was able to raise my score significantly. That's why I feel bad for my parents dropping $1,000 dollars on those SAT classes, but I understand that they had the best intentions. Make it evident to your parents that you are indeed trying the best you can.

—MICHAEL
SAN DIEGO, CALIFORNIA
SAT/ACT SCORES: 2190
UNDECIDED

THERE ARE FEW FRIENDS in my group that really value the importance of these tests as I do. ACT and SAT take a backseat to partying and booze. Only a few of my friends truly practice or review in order to ensure a better score. Few of them even took the ACT other than the required school date in April. I got a 33 on the ACT; my closest friend got a 25. Their average was around a 21/22. I know that these friends of mine have qualities other than their intelligence or book-smartness going for them. Of course I would like it if they put forth more effort to succeed, but that lies in their hands, not mine.

> —*JAKE M. KENNEDY*
> *HICKORY HILLS, ILLINOIS*
> *SAT/ACT SCORES: 2100/33*
> *UNIVERSITY OF SOUTHERN CALIFORNIA*

• • • • • • • •

WHAT MADE ME STUDY the hardest for the ACT exam was not my conceited parents or my desire to make them proud of me. I wanted an extremely high test score because my two best girlfriends and I made a bet that, whoever scored the highest would never have to pay when we went out—for the whole summer before college. Plus, the winner was to receive a weekly allowance of ten dollars per loser. We were women of our word, so we took that bet.

> —*MARIJOSEPHE BROWN*
> *PLANO, ILLINOIS*
> *SAT/ACT SCORES: 1260/24*
> *ELMHURST COLLEGE*

• • • • • • • •

MOST HIGH SCHOOLS ARE HELPFUL. After all, great scores also reflect well on the school!

> —*N.*
> *NEW YORK, NEW YORK*

ARE SCHOOL-BASED SAT CLASSES WORTH IT?

More and more high schools are offering SAT prep classes before or after school. Are these classes worth taking?

PRO	CON
School-based classes are usually less expensive than out-of-school alternatives.	To put it bluntly, classes in school aren't always great. There are exceptions, but the courses offered by schools are often low-cost, low-quality alternatives.
Because the classes are at school and take place before or after regular classes, they're usually more convenient.	If taught by high school teachers, those teachers may not have a lot of experience with SAT-specific content or strategies.
Usually in-school classes require less of a time commitment.	Longer and more intense out-of-school classes may provide better results.
It's more fun to take a class with your friends.	School classes usually don't group students by ability level, leading to a one-size-fits-all approach.

HOW SCHOOLS CAN HELP ... OR NOT

AS SOON AS I WALKED INTO THE SCHOOL on the first day of my junior year, walls were displayed with bulletin boards and posters about the ACT. About once a week, each homeroom teacher was required to give a section sample of the ACT. We had pep rallies and special after-school sessions.

—*KEVISHA ITSON*
CHICAGO, ILLINOIS
SAT/ACT SCORES: 20
UNIVERSITY OF ILLINOIS, URBANA-CHAMPAIGN

• • • • • • • • •

MY SCHOOL IS VERY ACT-INTENSIVE. They don't really care about the SAT. It's kind of a paradox because, while they expected me to do well on the SAT, the teachers did very little to ensure that I made the scores. I think they expected me to do well based on how I had been performing in the classroom. I went into both tests with very little prep.

—*N.R.*
MEMPHIS, TENNESSEE
SAT/ACT SCORES: 1260/35
UNDECIDED

• • • • • • • • •

MY AP ENGLISH TEACHER DOES QUITE a bit of review, mainly with vocabulary words. It's one of the hardest things for me to do, so getting graded on them at school gives me extra incentive to study them.

—*TIM*
PHOENIX, ARIZONA
SAT/ACT SCORES: 2130
UNDECIDED

• • • • • • • • •

MY SCHOOL OFFERED CLASSES ON THE SAT and the teachers stayed after school to help us study. I don't think I would have gotten a high enough score to get into any college without my high school's preparatory class.

—*CESAR OCAMPO*
MONTEREY PARK, CALIFORNIA

MY SCHOOL ALSO ENCOURAGES FRESHMEN to take the SAT, and the incentive is that for freshmen, it's free. I'm sure that attracts parents more than it does the students. A lot of people say that taking it as a freshman is too soon, but it doesn't count for freshmen, and it's free, so why not? Basically, they just get the actual testing experience without having to pay anything or have it go on their record. My school also has mock SAT tests from time to time on campus. It's helpful in giving you an idea of how you'd do on the actual test.

—MICHAEL
SAN DIEGO, CALIFORNIA
SAT/ACT SCORES: 2190
UNDECIDED

- - - - - - - -

MY SCHOOL ALWAYS BECAME HYSTERICAL around ACT time. I don't know why, because it wasn't as if the school was judged on the ACT scores. We hired outside companies to prep students, teachers stayed behind to prep students, even parents who had scored a 22 or higher were asked to volunteer with the students twice a week, with free sandwiches as an incentive.

—MARIJOSEPHE BROWN
PLANO, ILLINOIS
SAT/ACT SCORES: 1260/24
ELMHURST COLLEGE

- - - - - - - -

SAT WORKSHOPS AT THE SCHOOL: Whether or not SAT workshops are helpful for you really depends on your learning style. At my school, the workshops were held in auditoriums with tons of kids and one teacher using an overhead projector. It was very easy to get distracted and start talking to my friend next to me instead of paying attention.

—ELIZABETH
MADISON, WISCONSIN
SAT/ACT SCORES: 1260/28
UNIVERSITY OF SOUTHERN CALIFORNIA

WHEN I WAS IN HIGH SCHOOL, there was a lot of pressure to do well on the ACT. This was because my school was known for producing an average ACT score of 25, and having top Illinois colleges scouting students. I remember in my sophomore year, there was a pledge all students had to sign. It was basically a promise to study every day through reading, watching educational programs or visiting some educational place. To be honest, I felt that I had to live up to my promise. Now, I didn't study every day, but mostly everything that I did that was fun, like ice-skating, or watching a film, I tried to learn something from. It worked: I got a 27.

    —CARLA
    CHICAGO, ILLINOIS
    SAT/ACT SCORES: 27
    UNIVERSITY OF GEORGIA

• • • • • • • • •

I DON'T REALLY THINK MY SCHOOL helped us prepare as well as they could have. Also, they should have had us preparing for the ACT, or at least thinking about it more, during our sophomore and junior years.

    —JENNIFER STEWART
    MURFREESBORO, TENNESSEE
    SAT/ACT SCORES: 25
    MIDDLE TENNESSEE STATE UNIVERSITY

• • • • • • • • •

MY SCHOOL DOESN'T OFFER ANY SPECIFIC classes for prep, but in both my English and math classes we did sample tests and learned some strategies. The counseling department does help a little, with information about registering and tips on the ACT vs. the SAT. We had a workshop last year on the PSAT, which was helpful for the SAT. Also, next week there's this thing on the SAT essay, which is a workshop held by a test prep company.

    —NEIL SHAH
    ENCINO, CALIFORNIA
    SAT/ACT SCORES: 2230
    UNDECIDED

MY PARENTS WERE REALLY involved in the whole process, and I am so grateful for that. They made sure that I had all of the resources needed to succeed. Also, since they already went through all of this with my older sister, they knew which company offered the best courses. In this process, teenagers have to let go and realize that their parents know best. For the most part, they have gone through the college process themselves. For me, it wasn't that hard to ask my parents for help. They are really involved in my education as well, always asking about my grades, homework, so the SATs and ACTs were no different for me. My parents have always told me to strive to do my best, so they wanted to give me as many resources as possible.

—*LAUREN*
POTOMAC, MARYLAND
SAT/ACT SCORES: 33
CORNELL UNIVERSITY

My parents forced me to study, study and study. They were pretty annoying, but I get pretty lazy sometimes, so I guess the nagging was a necessary evil.

—*AMAR PANJWANI*
APPLE VALLEY, CALIFORNIA
UNDECIDED

• • • • • • • •

I THINK THAT YOUR PARENTS' support has a lot to do with how you do on the SAT. If your parents are going to get really mad if you don't do well, then the pressure is really hard to deal with. But, if you have your parents to back you up 100 percent then the pressure is really not that big of an issue. If you find that your parents are putting too much pressure on you about the SAT, talk to them about it as soon as possible.

—*ANONYMOUS*
BURBANK, CALIFORNIA
SAT/ACT SCORES: 870/19
PEPPERDINE UNIVERSITY

Studying with
your friends
can be really
helpful if your
friends are as
serious as you
are.

—*Tim*
  Phoenix, Arizona
  SAT/ACT
  Scores: 2130
  UNDECIDED

My parents are very detached from my college search. It seems like a lot of parents know their kids' stats and everything, but my parents came from another country so they're not familiar with the whole system. It's good and it's bad. It's kind of a breath of fresh air since everyone at school (including my teachers) expects me to go to a top-notch Ivy League school, but my parents are all about me doing the best I can. Sometimes it's frustrating because they don't understand the magnitude and importance of the whole process. They don't understand the level of achievement that I've reached. I would definitely try to impress upon your parents that yes, it is a big deal, and that yes, sometimes you do need help with it. The good news is that I've pretty much got everything under control.

—*N.R.*
  Memphis, Tennessee
  SAT/ACT Scores: 1260/35
  UNDECIDED

I have the type of parents who show no mercy when it comes to test scores, good grades and graduating on time, though neither of them had ever taken the ACTs. However, they both completed college and felt whatever minimum requirements to get into college should be exceeded. It was the family way. Anything below a 30 was unacceptable and I would have to suffer daily lectures of how spoiled modern children are today and how they worked and went to school. I didn't get harsh lectures, but I did get the silent treatment for about a day and a half, until my parents humbled themselves enough to say "good job."

—*Marijosephe Brown*
  Plano, Illinois
  SAT/ACT Scores: 1260/24
  Elmhurst College

DEALING WITH PARENTS

They mean well. They really do. But sometimes parents can add an unbelievable amount of stress to the SAT process. Here are some tips for dealing with them:

- Take ownership of your own SAT preparation. Think of it from their perspective: their pride and joy is taking an important test, and they want to do everything in their power to make sure you get the highest possible score. If they see that you're signing up, studying, etc., on your own, they'll realize they don't need to worry and nag.

- Give them updates. Keep your parents in the loop about your SAT plans, and be loud and obvious about all of the studying you're doing.

- Manage expectations. It's tough to know in advance how you'll do on the SAT. But when you do have an idea of how you're doing based on practice exams (and the PSAT), you should tell your parents. If your parents understand your possible college admissions outcomes, it will spare them an emotional roller coaster (and spare you the fallout!).

MY MOM HELPED ME OUT with one thing. I was good at math (scoring above 700 was a walk in the park for me), but I had some issues with the Verbal sections, especially with vocabularies. So every day, I handed my mom a list of new words and she'd make vocabulary cards for me. Soon, I had a boxful of cards to study with, and they really helped a lot.

—*SOLOMON CHANG*
PROVIDENCE, RHODE ISLAND
SAT/ACT SCORES: 1410
COLLEGE OF WILLIAM AND MARY

• • • • • • • •

MY PARENTS STARTED PLANNING for me to take the SAT the day I was born. I didn't know it at the time, but now I realize that all of those verbal and math software programs they've been buying me throughout my lifetime were preparatory classes in disguise. I guess I owe them a lot because I felt really prepared for the SAT and I barely studied at all.

—*ASHLEY*
SAN FRANCISCO, CALIFORNIA
SAT/ACT SCORES: 2100
UNIVERSITY OF SOUTHERN CALIFORNIA

• • • • • • • •

THERE WAS PRESSURE TO perform better than my American friends because they grew up prepping for the SATs, and they just knew that my score would be low. I wanted to prove them wrong, and I did. Plus, in order to get into the coveted engineering program at my college, I had to score above average on the Math session.

—*TSHINO KANKWENDA*
MONTREAL, CANADA

REMEMBER THIS NAME

In 1999, Vinodhini (Vino) Vasudevan made national headlines as the first 12-year-old to earn a perfect score on the SAT.

Tricks and Strategies: Tips for Besting the Test

C ontrary to popular opinion, there are no tricks or secret strategies that will help you ace the SAT. Sure, there are some methods for answering questions that may work better than others. But to answer an SAT math question, you'll almost always need to understand the math underlying the question; to answer a question about a reading passage, you'll most likely need to have read and understood the passage; to deal with a grammar issue, you'll need to understand the basic principles of English grammar.

That doesn't mean that there isn't a right way and a wrong way to answer each question. Everyone knows people who are "good at taking tests," regardless of how well they do in their classes at school. What separates a good test taker from a poor one? Good test takers *understand the types of questions they're likely to face, know ways to answer them that might not be obvious simply from the subject matter, and can move efficiently through the test.*

Good test takers understand what the test writers are looking for, so they can avoid unnecessary work that creates confusion and wastes time. They don't struggle to use long vocabulary words in the SAT essay when graders are mostly looking for organization and good writing. They don't let themselves use complicated trigonometry to solve a math problem when they know that the SAT doesn't test trig and thus there must be an easier way.

In this chapter, we asked successful SAT takers for their best strategies.

I'M A SLOW READER so I really had to strategize when it came to the Reading part. I had to use short cuts; one of the things I did was read the questions relating to the passage, then go back and read. Then I knew what I was looking for. Otherwise I would have gotten bogged down thinking every detail was important. It's also really important to follow the clock. You should bring your own clock; the clock was behind me and it was distracting to keep looking back at it.

> —*HALEY*
> *PETALUMA, CALIFORNIA*
> *SAT/ACT SCORES: 1750*
> *UNIVERSITY OF CALIFORNIA, DAVIS*

. . . .

AS FAR AS TIMEKEEPING GOES, I say: practice, practice, practice! Timekeeping was my biggest trouble spot when I took the SAT. I had to do countless sections from practice tests (and time myself!) before getting the timing right, especially in the Math section. Try to pace yourself.

> —*CHRISTINE TODD*
> *VERO BEACH, FLORIDA*
> *SAT/ACT SCORES: 2250*
> *NORTHWESTERN UNIVERSITY*

. . . .

I DID REALLY WELL ON THE VERBAL, but I still had to pay close attention to the trick questions. On the sentence completion questions there would often be answer choices that sounded like the right word. You have to be alert to these tricks because there are so many words that sound the same and even have almost all of the same letters. There are points in the test where you just get so tired and can easily fall victim to the slight variances.

> —*EMMA*
> *WASHINGTON, D.C.*
> *SAT/ACT SCORES: 1890*
> *PITZER COLLEGE*

Watch out for the SAT "sucker answer." On multiple-choice tests, there is always the right answer and the sucker choice. I always fell for the latter.

—*C.B.*
NEW YORK,
NEW YORK
SAT/ACT
SCORES: 1250
SYRACUSE
UNIVERSITY

HEADLINES
Best Advice and Top Tips

- Use any extra time you have to double-check your work.
- The SAT is a marathon: Give it your all. At the end of the test, you should have nothing left in the tank.
- Finish all the questions you know the answers to as quickly as possible. Then go back and tackle the ones that gave you trouble.

The smartest thing to do during the SAT is to never trust your gut instinct; the test-makers prey on that!

—NA YOUNG
  PLAINSBORO,
  NEW JERSEY
  CARNEGIE
  MELLON
  UNIVERSITY

ON THE VERBAL SECTION, they will throw in words you may never have heard of. But don't worry; if you think the question through, you will find that you can arrive at the correct answer using other techniques (process of elimination, derivations from other languages, etc.). One SAT teacher always reminded me that the SAT questions are not measures of memory but rather puzzles to take apart. If you practice enough questions (in both Math and Verbal), you will realize that the reasoning is the same but the actual words and numbers may differ. Study books teach you tricks along with a general review of math and verbal skills.

—BETH LORI WECKSELL
  GREAT NECK, NEW YORK
  SAT/ACT SCORES: 1370
  TUFTS UNIVERSITY

FOR CRITICAL READING, break the reading into short chunks—paragraphs at a time—and answer the questions specific to each paragraph that you go through. This way, you don't forget what you read and you save time: If you were to read the whole reading selection all the way through first, you'd find that you'd have to go back into it when you were looking at the questions. By doing the questions in chunks as you're reading it, it's still fresh in your head. Princeton Review has this method of not reading the passage at all and just going straight to the questions and reading whatever is specific to the question, but that totally didn't work for me. It actually made my score go down, but I know some people who swear by that method. The best thing to do would be to experiment to see what works best for you.

—*MICHAEL*
SAN DIEGO, CALIFORNIA
SAT/ACT SCORES: 2190
UNDECIDED

❝ Expect that you won't know all the answers when you take the SAT. Don't put too much pressure on yourself. For me, the hardest part was to skip questions that I was unsure of and move on. ❞

—*CINDY*
NEW YORK, NEW YORK
NEW YORK UNIVERSITY

Use your calculator to go back and check your math if you have time at the end. Use every minute to double check.

—MICHAL ROSENOER
CORTE MADERA,
CALIFORNIA
SAT/ACT
SCORES: 2220
UNIVERSITY OF
CALIFORNIA,
BERKELEY

SOMETIMES A PASSAGE in Critical Reading will bore you to tears and you'll want to come back to the whole thing later. But if you walk in with enthusiasm, thinking "these passages are sure gonna be fun to read," as I do, it's usually not a problem. The passages usually *are* fun to read, and when I studied with others the passages occasionally sparked good discussions.

—JESSICA
BOCA RATON, FLORIDA
SAT/ACT SCORES: 2390
CALIFORNIA INSTITUTE OF TECHNOLOGY

* * * * * * * *

THE CRITICAL READING SECTION is totally crackable if you can learn to perform a series of binary tests—that is, you look at an answer choice, then look for evidence. Since everything is there in the passage, you can easily get the right choice by eliminating the wrong ones. Same thing is true for the sentence completions, especially the two-blankers. You don't need to know the right word to figure out which ones are wrong.

—ASHRAF EASSA
WINDAM, NEW HAMPSHIRE
SAT/ACT SCORES: 2040
MASSACHUSETTS INSTITUTE OF TECHNOLOGY

* * * * * * * *

THE TEST MAKERS ARE GOING to try to fool you. For example, they usually give you two answers that could be right. However, there's always a better answer. They will make your brain go in circles, but when in doubt, use your gut instincts. No matter how long you sit there (meanwhile, wasting precious test time) you will not understand it any better. Eliminate two or more of the answers and take your best guess.

—CASEY PONTIOUS
LOCUST GROVE, OKLAHOMA
FREE WILL BAPTIST BIBLE COLLEGE

LOCATION IS EVERYTHING

IT'S IMPORTANT TO PICK A GOOD LOCATION to take your test, and the only way to figure out which places are better is to talk to upperclassmen who have taken the test before you. The first time I took the test I had to wait in line to get in and get my seat; the test started late and the people were noisy. The second time I took it, I asked friends where they took theirs and I had a much better experience and my scores were higher.

> —*A.C.*
> *BERKELEY, CALIFORNIA*
> *SAT/ACT SCORES: 1800*
> *UNIVERSITY OF CALIFORNIA, BERKELEY*

• • • • • • • • •

I SIGNED UP LATE FOR MY TEST, so I couldn't get the location I wanted. I ended up taking my exam in a place where I noticed there was a lot of cheating going on. It made me really uncomfortable especially when I realized there were people trying to look at my answers. I never said anything because I was scared, but I also ended up canceling my scores because I could not concentrate at all and I knew I wouldn't do well. The next time I signed up, I made sure to do it well in advance.

> —*ASHLEY*
> *SAN FRANCISCO, CALIFORNIA*
> *SAT/ACT SCORES: 2100*
> *UNIVERSITY OF SOUTHERN CALIFORNIA*

THREE THINGS TO REMEMBER

Do not let yourself get distracted during the test. Just ignore the guy next to you who is picking his nose with his pencil while talking to himself.

Make sure you're filling out the correct section of the Scantron sheet for that section of the test!

As soon as you're done with one part of the test, don't worry about it any more; not only are you not allowed to go back, but it's over, so concentrate on doing the best you can on this section.

—TIMOTHY MICHAEL COOPER
NEW YORK, NEW YORK
YALE UNIVERSITY

PEOPLE ARE TEMPTED to answer all the questions in a multiple-choice test because the answer is right there! Because wrong answers count against the test taker, and blank ones don't, it is far better to leave some blank.

—CINDY
NEW YORK, NEW YORK
NEW YORK UNIVERSITY

IT IS OKAY TO LEAVE SOME OF the answers blank. On high school tests, you're told to answer every question. But with the SAT, if you cannot make a good guess and are absolutely clueless, then leave it blank. It goes against what I was taught, but it helped to relieve the stress by allowing me to focus my time on questions I knew the answer to or could make a good guess on. I scored much higher on the SAT when I left a few blank than when I answered every single question.

—*LAURA BOUTWELL*
WINCHESTER, VIRGINIA
SAT/ACT SCORES: 1410
COLLEGE OF WILLIAM AND MARY

• • • • • • • •

IF YOU COME ACROSS a really difficult section, just relax, don't stress about it. The Math and Writing were straightforward for me, but the Reading Comprehension was challenging. I just can't seem to read and comprehend what I'm reading at the same time. I studied reading comprehension the most, but during the test, even though I wasn't getting it, I didn't stress over it. If I had stressed over it, I would have messed up on the other sections.

—*JESSICA*
DALLAS, TEXAS
RICE UNIVERSITY

• • • • • • • •

AFTER TAKING THE SAT the first time, I realized I should not have spent so much time thinking about certain questions that I was unsure of, since when you get the answer wrong you lose more points compared to just leaving it blank. On multiple-choice questions, if you can eliminate one answer, guess.

—*ANONYMOUS*
UNDECIDED

Focus on each section as an individual part. It does you no good to worry about the Math while you're working on the Reading.

—*REBECCA*
ST. LOUIS,
MISSOURI
WASHINGTON
UNIVERSITY

ALL QUESTIONS COUNT EQUALLY, so don't worry if you don't get to the hardest ones. In fact, if you know you're not going to get to every question, just focus on the easier questions (the ones closer to the beginning of each section), since they count as much as the ones toward the end of the section. As you get closer to the end of one section of a particular type of question, the answers almost always get less and less obvious. So if you see a question in the last half or especially the last third of a section of questions and the answer jumps out at you, that's almost definitely the wrong answer.

—*TIMOTHY MICHAEL COOPER*
NEW YORK, NEW YORK
YALE UNIVERSITY

" I circled all the answers right on the test booklet and then went back later and transferred my answers to the answer sheet. That way, I stayed in the 'answering mode' there was no going back and forth wondering, 'What number was I on?' "

—*TORI*
BIRMINGHAM, ALABAMA
SAT/ACT SCORES: 2300/34

PC ADVICE

Remember that the correct answers on the SATs are always politically correct! For instance, in a passage about Native Americans (perhaps, "What attitude does the author have towards Native Americans?"), let's say the answer choices are: a) They are a primitive, uneducated race; b) Their culture is interesting and worth learning about; c) Their craft skills are second-rate in comparison to our modern industrial skills; and d) They are a beautiful people with important social and religious beliefs. Right away, you can rule out choices a and c because they put Native Americans in a bad light by calling them primitive and uneducated and by downplaying the level and importance of their skills. Your choice between the remaining answers, B and D, will depend on the specifics in the passage you have read.

—CHRISTINE TODD
VERO BEACH, FLORIDA
SAT/ACT SCORES: 2250
NORTHWESTERN UNIVERSITY

SAT STRATEGY I: KEEP YOUR OWN TIME

Don't rely on the wall clock or on the proctors who are supposed to remember to call out time. They have the final word, of course, but it's dangerous to rely on a clock that you may not be able to see well or on monitors who may forget to call out warnings. Besides, a wall clock with hands isn't the best way to time a 25-minute test section. If a section starts at, say, 9:48, you'll practically have to do a math problem each time you look at the clock just to figure out how much time is left!

First and foremost, never panic!

—*BETH LORI WECKSELL GREAT NECK, NEW YORK SAT/ACT SCORES: 1370 TUFTS UNIVERSITY*

WHENEVER I SKIPPED A QUESTION, I used different symbols (like stars, circles, etc.) to mark the questions I had no clue on, and the ones I thought I might be able to figure out when I looked over the test again. That way, if I had only a few minutes left in the testing session, I could focus on the questions that I felt I could work out, instead of wasting time on questions that I knew I didn't know how to do.

—*LAURA BOUTWELL WINCHESTER, VIRGINIA SAT/ACT SCORES: 1410 COLLEGE OF WILLIAM AND MARY*

I DIDN'T SPEND TOO MUCH TIME on one question. If I found myself staring at the question, and getting stuck, I just marked the letter C, and put a question mark in the test booklet so I could come back to it if I had time.

—*ZAKIA SIPP CHICAGO, ILLINOIS SAT/ACT SCORES: 28 CHICAGO STATE UNIVERSITY*

SAT STRATEGY II: DON'T WASTE TIME WITH MULTIPLE-CHOICE GUESSING SHORTCUTS

The SAT is put together by psychometricians, who design multiple-choice tests for a living. You can't outsmart them. Just because C hasn't come up for a while doesn't mean its due. Even more intelligent strategies almost never work. There is a big difference between the SAT and tests in school, where teachers who are better at history than writing tests will commonly put together questions that are easy to outwit.

WHENEVER I TEST, I mark the answer in the book, and cross out whatever I eliminate in the book. This helps keep my choices in elimination more visible. After every five questions, I transfer all circled responses into the answer sheet to save time spent going back and forth between the sheet and the booklet. When time starts to run out, though, I fill the bubble as soon as I get the answer. To skip questions, I circle the number and move on. I can't afford to waste any time on something I have to think too long on. Once I'm done with the section, I go back to the circled problems and can usually figure them out by then. Sometimes simply having time on other questions can clear your mind to tackle the hard question you skipped with full force.

—JOSEPH ANDA
LITTLE ROCK, ARKANSAS
SAT/ACT SCORES: 2300
UNDECIDED

SAT STRATEGY III: SKIP THE TOUGHEST QUESTIONS

Unless you're planning to get a nearly perfect SAT score, there will probably be a handful of questions that you should skip. Some test takers will want to skip as many as half of the questions. Giving up on questions is of course never ideal, but on a very difficult, time-pressured test it can be a valuable strategy. Skipping questions means that you run out of time on the *hardest* questions (the ones you skipped) instead of simply the ones at the end, which may or may not be hard for you.

ON THE READING PORTION, always look at the first word in the answer options. Based on that, you can learn what the answer is. For example, most test answers begin with the words, "inform," "guide," "entertain," and "persuade," followed by less important words in the sentence. But the first words are the most important.

—*MARIJOSEPHE BROWN*
PLANO, ILLINOIS
SAT/ACT SCORES: 1260/24
ELMHURST COLLEGE

• • • • • • • •

EXPECT THAT THE SAT is a long test with time restrictions. When I was preparing for the SATs, I never actually timed the sections. Thus, when I took the actual test, I felt rushed and ran out of time. Prep with time to have an understanding to budget the questions!

—*C.B.*
NEW YORK, NEW YORK
SAT/ACT SCORES: 1250
SYRACUSE UNIVERSITY

SAT STRATEGY IV: MAINTAIN YOUR FOCUS

The SAT is a marathon, not a sprint. This may be the most important test you ever take, and you should treat it as such. Hunker down over your answer sheet, move quickly, and answer each question as if it were the most important thing in the world. When you leave the SAT you should have no gas left in your tank. If you can still think straight, that means you didn't work hard enough.

SOMETHING I LEARNED from my SAT tutor was that the test is not looking for specific skills in math, reading, or grammar; rather the sections are testing one's ability to understand what the question is asking and logically finding a way to the answer. I was too focused on trying to brush up on math formulas and lessons that I had taken years before and learning a bunch of new vocabulary words. However, you only need very basic skill levels for the sections on the SAT, and once you start looking at the questions for what they are asking instead of worrying about what formula you have to use to get the answer or definitions you have to know, the answers will come much more easily.

—*TERRAHNEY WILSON*
LITHONIA, GEORGIA
SAT/ACT SCORES: 1950
UNDECIDED

SAT STRATEGY V: KNOW HOW THE QUESTION ORDER AND TIMING WORKS

Most of the SAT sections are 25 minutes long. Others are 20 or 10 minutes long. Know not only those times, but also how you should be progressing through each section. How long does it typically take you to do the sentence completion questions? To read and complete an eight-question reading passage? To do the last five math problems?

THE SAT TEST MAKERS TRY to confuse you by making a lot of "plausible distractors" in the answers. Many times, more than one or two answers seem correct. Also, some questions almost seem too easy and they are. Don't look too much into the question if it seems too easy because it probably is, so don't second-guess yourself.

—*ALAINA SILVERMAN*
ELKINS PARK, PENNSYLVANIA
SAT/ACT SCORES: 1210
UNIVERSITY OF MARYLAND

• • • • • • • •

THE TOUGHEST QUESTIONS are the ones with incorrect answers that appear to be the best choice at first glance if you are not paying attention to the remaining choices available. These questions usually take just a little more focus and concentration than the rest, but by re-reading and focusing in on key words in the question, you should be able to choose the correct answer.

—*ANONYMOUS*
NEW YORK, NEW YORK
NEW YORK UNIVERSITY

SAT STRATEGY VI: TAKE SHORTCUTS

No, guessing tricks don't work on the SAT. But that doesn't mean it's like any old test in school. On the SAT, only the right answer matters—no one is grading how you got to your answer, or whether you did a good enough job of showing your work. So don't write out every step to a math problem unless it's necessary. Feel free to test answers to see which ones work, ignoring the "proper" way of doing the problem. If you found an easy way to eliminate an answer, feel free to do so. And so forth.

THE FIRST TWO TIMES I took the test, I did leave some questions blank. But by the third take, I was more confident in my abilities to perform well on the test. As such, I didn't leave any blank. I could always eliminate some answers, and felt as though it was more beneficial to try to get the extra point, rather than lose a point and a quarter. My score increased significantly the third time around.

>   —*KEVIN WANDREI*
>   *ADAMS, MASSACHUSETTS*
>   *SAT/ACT SCORES: 1260/28*
>   *UNIVERSITY OF SOUTHERN CALIFORNIA*

• • • • • • • •

IF YOU SPEND MORE THAN two minutes on any question, you've spent too long. Go through the section and complete all the questions you know; those are guaranteed. Then go back and look over the ones that cause a little more trouble.

>   —*COLLEEN DAVIS*
>   *LEXINGTON, KENTUCKY*
>   *SAT/ACT SCORES: 2150/31*
>   *WASHINGTON UNIVERSITY IN ST. LOUIS*

SAT STRATEGY VII: GO AHEAD AND GUESS

While students are typically told *not* to guess randomly on the SAT, on average the wrong answer penalties will exactly cancel out the points you get from correct guesses. So if you have no clue on a question, you can either guess or not guess. And if you can eliminate even one answer, guessing is a no-brainer. Just don't spend time on crazy guessing theories, which as we've already discussed simply don't work.

On the ACT there is *no* guessing penalty, so you must fill in absolutely every bubble.

There are a lot of ambiguous questions on the SAT in which two answers are similar and both seem to fit. When you are stuck, eliminate the extremes.

—*Yueyue Guo*
Cumberland,
Rhode Island
SAT/ACT
Scores: 2220
UNDECIDED

THIS IS WHAT WORKED FOR ME: I just dove into the multiple-choice questions and came back to any I had trouble with. Another big thing: with the Reading part of the test, I recommend that you read the questions *before* reading the excerpt. This saved me a lot of time. Also, always look carefully at the wording of the question. Take special notice of the words "except," "only," "true," "false," etc.

—*Ryan Bates*
Hudson, Wisconsin

• • • • • • • •

DON'T SPEND TOO MUCH TIME on each question. If you don't know the answer in a minute, just leave it blank. This really helped me because I found that I was able to get through the entire test and answer the questions that I knew really quickly and go back to the more difficult ones.

—*Elisa Viera*
Whittier, California

I WAS TAUGHT IN MY PREP classes never to read the entire section of a reading passage because it wastes time, and since the students are so focused on finishing before the time runs out, we would forget the important points of the passage anyway. I also answered the questions that had underlined words first, since they were mostly definition questions, where the answer could be found directly in the passage. Doing these two things allowed me to finish before time was up. Plus, I scored the highest in the Reading, even though that is my all time worst subject.

—*KEVISHA ITSON*
CHICAGO, ILLINOIS
SAT/ACT SCORES: 20
UNIVERSITY OF ILLINOIS, URBANA-CHAMPAIGN

" The questions get harder as you go so I worked from the bottom up. As for the bottom questions, which were harder, I never picked "None of the above" or "All of the above." Those answers are just too easy for those tricky ones at the bottom. "

—*MICHAL ROSENOER*
CORTE MADERA, CALIFORNIA
SAT/ACT SCORES: 2220
UNIVERSITY OF CALIFORNIA, BERKELEY

Consider

THE WORDINGS OF SOME OF the questions are tricky and the answers are so similar to one another sometimes, that you tend to second-guess yourself. It's usually your best bet to just stick with your initial answer. And don't fixate on a question if you just don't get it. Move on and don't waste time or energy if you can move along to other questions. If you have time, go back to them at the end.

—*ELANA JUDITH SYRTASH*
NEW YORK, NEW YORK
YESHIVA UNIVERSITY

The Test: Critical Reading Section

Critical Reading is probably the most difficult part of the SAT for which to prepare. Your vocabulary, which is tested in the sentence completion questions at the beginning of each Critical Reading section, is very difficult to expand considerably in just a few months (even if you could memorize a few thousand vocabulary words in that amount of time, it most likely wouldn't be worth it). Similarly, passage-based reading doesn't test discrete concepts but instead measures your ability to read quickly and understand what you've read. Whatever your reading ability, it's probably not going to change much while you study for the SAT.

What can you do to get ready for the Critical Reading section? The students we interviewed in this section had some excellent suggestions, some of which you might be able to incorporate into your *own study and test-taking plan. While you might not be able to become a vocabulary master between now and the SAT, you can certainly check out some of the advice here about how and when to study vocabulary words, and where to find words that you're likely to see again on the SAT.*

For the reading passages, it seems as though there are dozens of approaches, not only to answering questions, but to reading the passages in the first place. Why commit early to one method? Instead, review the advice given here and experiment until you find the system that works best for you.

MAKE SURE TO ANSWER all of the questions about one passage before continuing to the next passage. You may think that you will remember everything once you return to the first passage towards the end of your allotted time. But you will be much better off if you complete each passage's block of questions in the same group, as opposed to mixing them up with other passages.

—*CHRISTINE TODD*
VERO BEACH, FLORIDA
SAT/ACT SCORES: 2250
NORTHWESTERN UNIVERSITY

WHEN READING LONG PASSAGES, look ahead to the questions for the section and underline the parts of the paragraph that apply to each question. This way, when you read through it the first time, you'll pay special attention to the underlined parts, and when you are looking between the paragraph and the questions, the underlined portions catch your eye much faster, saving you many precious seconds.

—*ALLISON FOREMAN*
COLUMBIA, SOUTH CAROLINA
SAT/ACT SCORES: 1520/34
CLEMSON UNIVERSITY

THE READING SECTION GAVE me the most trouble. I was so worried about not focusing enough to understand what I was reading that I really didn't give the material a chance to captivate me. It's important to release yourself of all the anxiety of failure, and just breathe, then read for the enjoyment of it, not thinking about how important it is to understand. If you do that, then you won't be reading word for word, but as a whole.

—*JENNIFER STEWART*
MURFREESBORO, TENNESSEE
SAT/ACT SCORES: 25
MIDDLE TENNESSEE STATE UNIVERSITY

Reading comprehension was my least favorite section of the SAT!

—*DREW SILVERMAN*
ELKINS PARK,
PENNSYLVANIA
SAT/ACT
SCORES: 1410
SYRACUSE
UNIVERSITY

HEAD**LINES**
Best Advice and Top Tips

- Vocabulary doesn't count as much on the new SAT, so don't spend too much of your time studying for it.
- Finish each Reading Comprehension section as quickly as possible. If you fall behind, you'll have to tackle your next section that much faster.

THE **CRITICAL READING SECTION** was the most difficult for me, in both the sentence completions and passages. For the sentence completions, it helped most to study vocabulary cards, and even though it took a while to get all the words down, they got a lot easier afterwards. I didn't study much for the passages, because they were so long and tedious. But I wish I had spent more time on them. If I was going to do it again I would have familiarized myself more with the types of questions, like "What does the author think about ..." I had most of my trouble reading so much into the passage when there was too little time. If I had gone over the more abstract questions and spent some time understanding where in the passage the answer came, I would have felt more comfortable answering those questions on test day.

—*DEEPTI KALLURI*
ACTON, MASSACHUSETTS
SAT/ACT SCORES: 2240
▥ *UNDECIDED*

To get in reading shape I checked out some books from the library on science and history. I would read a chapter and try to write down what I learned from the chapter. I think it helped me a little because when I had to read for the SAT I felt like I was more equipped to quickly catch the meaning.

—*Bryan*
Las Vegas, Nevada
SAT/ACT Scores: 2110
University of Southern California

. . . .

“ After skimming each passage, I answered those questions that referred back to particular lines of the passage before answering the one on the main point of the selection. ”

—*Brooke*
St. Louis, Missouri
Princeton University

. . . .

I am a big fan of reading the section first and then answering the questions, and other people prefer to read the questions first and then find the answers in the reading. I'm pretty good at retaining the information I read and recalling it to answer the questions. If I read the questions first it would be a big waste of time.

—*Elizabeth*
Denver, Colorado
SAT/ACT Scores: 2100
Claremont McKenna College

The reading comprehension stories on the SAT are unbelievably boring.

—*Bryan*
Las Vegas,
Nevada
SAT/ACT
Scores: 2110
University of
Southern
California

THE READING COMPREHENSION QUESTIONS assess both the general and the specific. To save time, I read the articles first for a general idea, keeping track of exactly where each topic is located. I found that when I was practicing for the test I had to go back to check details anyway, so it made sense not to try to retain everything on the first time through. Glancing at the questions first is also a good strategy.

—*Isaac*
Philadelphia, Pennsylvania
SAT/ACT Scores: 1300
Muhlenberg College

• • • • • • • •

THE READING SECTION OF THE SAT was very difficult. I struggled with this part at first, and this is one area where the course I took helped immensely. They taught me that I really did not need to read the whole thing or even understand it; I only had to focus on key phrases and parts. I found this to be kind of silly and a bad representation of scholastic aptitude, but I was able to have much more success on the section by following the course's advice.

—*Andrew Michael Rizzi*
Baldwin, New York
SAT/ACT Scores: 1390
Syracuse University

• • • • • • • •

I READ THE QUESTIONS FIRST and I put a dot next to all the lines referenced in the questions so when I read the parts I immediately answered that question, and continued reading. Then when you're done, you will have read the whole passage and can answer the questions that ask for tone and overall purpose, etc.

—*John*
Austin, Texas
SAT/ACT Scores: 2100
Boston University

WHAT'S TESTED IN THE SAT CRITICAL READING SECTION?

SAT Critical Reading includes both sentence completion questions and passage-based reading comprehension questions.

Sentence completion questions give you a sentence with one or two words missing. It's your job to decide which of five words— or pairs of words—work best in the sentence. For example, the sentence might be *Because Anne loved taking tests, on the morning of the SAT she was very* ____. Among the possible answer choices, *happy* might be the best choice. *Sad, angry, silly*, and *crazy* would all be incorrect.

This is the one part of the new SAT that still tests your vocabulary to a significant degree. While sentence-completion questions also test your ability to understand how sentences are structured, knowing the meanings of the words themselves will be essential to success on this part of the exam.

The other part of the Critical Reading section consists of passage-based reading questions. On this portion of the SAT, you read passages of various lengths and then answer questions about it. The questions can test the meaning of words in context, comprehension, or reasoning skills. Some types of passage-based reading questions ask about two related passages.

Passage-based reading is arguably the most time-intensive part of the SAT. For most students, the passage itself is simply too long to be read carefully in the time-allotted.

What really helped prepare me for the Reading and Writing sections were the books *Eats, Shoots & Leaves, The Elements of Style,* and *The Grammar Bible.*

—*JIAHAO*
SINGAPORE
SAT/ACT
SCORES: 2320
MIDDLEBURY
COLLEGE

THE COLLEGE BOARD PRIDES itself on being extremely open-minded and liberal. No correct answer in the Reading Comprehension section would ever be the least bit negative about women or minorities. Thus, any answer that could possibly be interpreted as saying that women or minorities are incapable of any achievement is definitely wrong. Correct answers in the Reading Comprehension section tend not to make blanket statements—that is, statements that use all-encompassing words like "all" or "always" or "every" when discussing a group. Therefore, an answer like "All British citizens were in complete agreement about how to handle the problem of colonization" is pretty much guaranteed to be incorrect.

—*TIMOTHY MICHAEL COOPER*
NEW YORK, NEW YORK
YALE UNIVERSITY

THE BEST WAY TO PREPARE for the Critical Reading section is to customize yourself to the type of questions they ask. Also, process of elimination is usually a pretty sure way to eliminate a couple of wrong answers in Reading Comprehension. The biggest challenge for me on the Reading Comprehension was just focusing on the selection without having my mind wander off. The topics were usually so boring that I would have to fly through it before the daydreaming kicked in. My best advice is to not be afraid to return to the selection to answer the questions, but at the same time you need to know roughly where you're looking. You can't afford to skim through the entire selection on every question.

—*DREW SILVERMAN*
ELKINS PARK, PENNSYLVANIA
SAT/ACT SCORES: 1410
SYRACUSE UNIVERSITY

READING THE WHOLE PASSAGE will stress you out. I just buckled down with the College Board's "Blue Book" and did all the tests, then went over all of the passages a lot of times to see if I could see any patterns in the Critical Reading. Quickly look over the passage first and then go to the questions. Just look at the first and last sentences of each paragraph. Reading the entire passage is just a waste of time.

—*ANONYMOUS*
WASHINGTON, D.C.
SAT/ACT SCORES: 2300
DARTMOUTH COLLEGE

"The first few times I took practice tests, I read the passages out loud with my mother right there. It really helped me absorb what I was reading. Eventually, I was able to do it, silently, without her."

—*ASHLEY*
SCOTTSDALE, ARIZONA
UNIVERSITY OF CALIFORNIA, LOS ANGELES

IN ORDER TO ACE the Reading Comprehension section you need to be able to read fast, retain the critical information, and know that the answer is in the passage.

—*JIKYU CHOI*
FAIR OAKS, CALIFORNIA
SAT/ACT SCORES: 2370
STANFORD UNIVERSITY

I AM REALLY WELL READ, so vocabulary comes pretty naturally to me; however the SAT does have a lot of words on it that just come out of left field. In order to learn them, I made flash cards, but with more than just the word and it's definition. I included the origin and the meanings of all the words separate parts. Also, while reviewing my flash cards, I always used the word I was studying in a sentence. I think this approach helps you learn, and make it more fun.

—*ANONYMOUS*
LAS VEGAS, NEVADA
SAT/ACT SCORES: 2300
VANDERBILT UNIVERSITY

• • • • • • • •

"The best way to succeed in the sentence completion section is just to be well read. Nothing improves vocabulary more than reading."

—*PHILLIP LAVIN*
MARIETTA, GEORGIA

• • • • • • • •

I DID BETTER WHEN I followed my own instincts rather than my tutor's directions, who told me to read the questions first and then read the actual passage. I took the SAT twice using that strategy and made about the same score each time. But on the third try, I did the opposite and I raised my score by 100 points in just that section.

—*JACK ALTMAN*
ST. LOUIS, MISSOURI
SAT/ACT SCORES: 2300/34
UNDECIDED

I ALWAYS READ FOR ENJOYMENT. But when I have to take tests that ask me to analyze what I read, I usually blow it because I don't rush. Sometimes the stories are good, and I forget I'm taking a test and read it again. So when I took the SATs, I ran out of time. If I had to do it all over again, I wouldn't have read the passage at all, just the questions, and gone back to find the answers.

> —*BETH HARVEY*
> *CHICAGO, ILLINOIS*
> *KENTUCKY WESLEYAN COLLEGE*

Critical Reading was the hardest part because it was the longest part.

> —*MARQUITA REESE*
> *CHICAGO, ILLINOIS*
> *SAT/ACT*
> *SCORES: 23*
> *CHICAGO STATE UNIVERSITY*

FOR THE CRITICAL READING SECTION, too many kids answer what they feel they want the answer to be, rather than choose the answer that portrays best what the text says. I did well by never giving an answer that wasn't clearly in the text. Historical passages really catch people off guard. They are confusing and they try to make the test taker answer the question with whatever coincides with their stance or their prior knowledge, rather than what the text says.

> —*NIKITA BIER*
> *PALOS VERDES, CALIFORNIA*
> *SAT/ACT SCORES: 2100*
> *STANFORD UNIVERSITY*

TOP CRITICAL READING STRATEGIES

DON'T FOCUS TOO MUCH ON VOCABULARY. Vocabulary is a part of the SAT, but it doesn't account for nearly as much of the test as it once did. It's probably not the best use of your time to study thousands of vocabulary words.

BROWSE OR SKIM THE PASSAGE BEFORE ANSWERING QUESTIONS. Most students will do best on the passage-based questions if they look through the passage before doing the questions. Sometimes it's tempting to do the questions first, looking back into the passage for answers. But using roughly one-third of your time quickly reading the passage—getting the important parts, looking for meaning, and establishing a roadmap in your head—will make the questions more understandable.

WATCH THE CLOCK. Timing is probably more important on the passage-based Reading portion of the SAT than anywhere else on the test. If you spend too much time on one passage, you'll do poorly on the next because, in addition to being forced to speed up, you won't have time to read the passage carefully before answering the questions.

The Test: Math Section

While you may think you know what to expect on the SAT Math section—and indeed, Math is the part of the SAT that most resembles what you've already done in school—there's a lot about SAT Math that can make it difficult and frustrating.

First, there's the time issue. The SAT is what's known as a "speeded" test, and that means that most students aren't expected to finish. You'll likely need to make decisions about where to focus your time and which questions to skip entirely.

Then, there's the tricky nature of the SAT Math section, which focuses primarily on arithmetic, algebra, and geometry—areas covered in school by most students long before they take the SAT. Instead of focusing entirely on the content of these subject areas, the SAT does *a terrific job of testing your "math IQ"—your ability to use math logic and reasoning to figure out problems you possibly haven't seen before.*

Sure, you need to know all of the basics. But there are plenty of students who get straight A's in math class who can't seem to get a handle on SAT Math. And vice versa—we all know someone who doesn't do well in school but manages to get a good math score on the SAT.

How do you study for SAT Math? Your best bet is to not only study math concepts, but also practice SAT questions, and think about timing and guessing strategy. Read here about what worked for others.

THE MATH SECTION is probably the easiest section on the test. I honestly think I could have taken the SAT Math section after the 9th grade and done fine on it.

—ANDREW TIMBERLAKE
BIRMINGHAM, ALABAMA
SAT/ACT SCORES: 2400
YALE UNIVERSITY

• • • • • • • •

"On one problem in the Math section, I was not getting an answer that matched any of the choices, so I moved on. I ended up only missing that one question, so it was probably a good idea not to get stuck on it."

—RAHUL RAJ MALIK
BIRMINGHAM, ALABAMA
SAT/ACT SCORES: 2260/35
UNDECIDED

• • • • • • • •

IF A SKETCH DOESN'T SAY, "Not drawn to scale," that means that it is drawn to scale. For geometry problems there is almost always a sketch. One time I couldn't figure out the answer, but I could tell that line Y was about 3 times the size of line X, so that was my answer. It was the difference between a 780 and an 800. So sometimes when you can't figure out a problem, the answer is right there in front of you in the picture.

—ANONYMOUS
ORADELL, NEW JERSEY
SAT/ACT SCORES: 2350
UNDECIDED

Best Advice and Top Tips

- You're better off skipping the hardest three questions instead of the three that happen to be last in the section.
- Quickly check your work after each question; it takes five seconds.

AFTER EVERY QUESTION, I quickly checked my work to make sure I didn't make careless mistakes; it only took about five seconds. Even doing this, I had about two to three minutes left over on all three sections to review. While I was taking practice tests for the Math section, I used to get a couple wrong, on average, each time. When I went back and reviewed my answers, I felt like a total idiot. I was committing careless mistakes that a 4th grader could probably recognize, and I decided this had to change to get the 800 I wanted. After some time, I discovered that the best time to check your work was right after you did the problem, because the question's information is fresh in your mind. Five to ten seconds of checking time should do it, and you still won't run out of time.

—*NEIL SHAH*
ENCINO, CALIFORNIA
SAT/ACT SCORES: 2230
UNDECIDED

YOU REALLY NEED TO LEARN to do math as quickly as possible, but error-free. Keeping myself from making simple arithmetic mistakes was the biggest challenge for me. In fact, what I did was blast through the Math section and leave myself enough time at the end to check my work all over again. Write everything down, and try not to add or subtract in your head. Every math problem has at least two numbers that you will need to work with. At the very least, write the two numbers down on a piece of paper. Seeing the problem on paper seemed to help me reduce errors.

> —PETER WILLIAM FINNOCCHIARO
> BALDWINSVILLE, NEW YORK
> SAT/ACT SCORES: 2300/32
> UNDECIDED

• • • • • • • • •

SOME OF THE QUESTIONS on the more difficult questions at the end of the Math sections had some strange concepts that I didn't understand. I tried working them out, but nothing came to mind. I think I could have explored more math areas, especially working with data and deriving answers from that. Since the test, I have seen very similar problems like the ones I found difficult. Hopefully I can find explanations for them and better understand them. Since my school didn't teach these concepts, I probably should have spent more time reviewing. I think I simply ran out of time. I was being pretty general about the whole test, and maybe I underestimated its difficulty. There are many different areas to study—geometry, data, and basic math—but even if you think you know your math, still go over everything. Don't get cocky and think you know the stuff.

> —AMAR PANJWANI
> APPLE VALLEY, CALIFORNIA
> UNDECIDED

You don't need to have taken calculus to do well on the SAT Math—just algebra and geometry; maybe algebra II.

—ANONYMOUS
ST. LOUIS,
MISSOURI
SAT/ACT SCORES:
2290/35
UNDECIDED

WHAT'S TESTED IN THE SAT MATHEMATICS SECTION?

SAT Math consists of multiple-choice questions and "student-produced response" questions that require you to bubble in your answer (e.g. "8.75") on a numerical grid. According to the College Board, the following areas are covered:

NUMBERS AND OPERATIONS: These questions include word problems, basic arithmetic, rational numbers, exponents, patterns and sequences, and similar concepts. This is where you'll find not only the SAT's simplest math number problems, but also complex story problems that test your understanding of percents, ratios, proportions, etc.

ALGEBRA AND FUNCTIONS: These questions cover a huge number of math concepts that you'll be expected to remember from school. Among the issues tested here are exponents, basic algebra, word problems with variables, equations of lines, functions questions that can include symbols, quadratic equations, various types of questions involving inequalities, systems of equations, and more.

GEOMETRY AND MEASUREMENT: These questions look at shapes and related concepts such as slope and similarity. While equations are provided at the beginning of each section, you'll still be asked to understand and calculate area (of circles, rectangles, and other shapes), volume, and other measurements. You'll also be tested on the Pythagorean Theorem, properties of triangles, slope, coordinate geometry, etc.

DATA ANALYSIS, STATISTICS, AND PROBABILITY: These questions focus mostly on interpreting data, statistical concepts (mean, median, mode), and probability.

I ALWAYS GET STRAIGHT A's in math but I had to work really hard to get my practice tests from 600 to 700. Functions were my biggest challenge on the Math section because my school did not put that much emphasis on them. There are only a few kinds of problems on the test and practicing will tell you which problems you need to work on, and that's when you seek help. It's more dedication than anything else.

—*TOM O'BRIEN*
SCRANTON, PENNSYLVANIA
SAT/ACT SCORES: 2160
UNDECIDED

* * * * * * * *

THE QUESTIONS GET HARDER as you go and this is especially true in the Math section. It's better to work from the top down for this section. Then you're starting with the easy ones; it makes you feel good and it goes quickly. If you work from the bottom up then you start with the hard ones and you end up spending more time on them. There's a greater chance you'll get them wrong, then you are rushed for the easy ones at the top, which would have been more of the sure things.

—*HALEY*
PETALUMA, CALIFORNIA
SAT/ACT SCORES: 1750
UNIVERSITY OF CALIFORNIA, DAVIS

* * * * * * * *

THE MATH ON THE SAT isn't like regular math. In a regular math problem, you might be asked to find the derivative, but the math questions on the SAT are really more like trick questions. They give you these intense word problems that require several steps to solve. The only way I was able to get through this was to take practice tests; for me it was just about getting used to the problems.

—*TIFFANY*
SHERMAN OAKS, CALIFORNIA
SAT/ACT SCORES: 1910
CLAREMONT MCKENNA COLLEGE

Review the algebra and geometry that you had in 8th grade. I didn't do that, and that's most of the math on the SAT.

—*Tori*
  Birmingham,
  Alabama
  SAT/ACT
  Scores: 2300/34

ONE OF THE MORE HELPFUL TIPS my tutor gave me was using process of elimination. When you look at your choices there is always going to be one that just can't be the answer. She also taught me to look carefully at each question and identify the first step, then the second step, and so on. I learned from her that I should approach math problems like I would a paper. When you write a paper you do an outline first, so you do the same type of thing for math.

—*Emma*
  Washington, D.C.
  SAT/ACT Scores: 1890
  Pitzer College

• • • • • • • •

ORGANIZING IS THE FIRST STEP. I used to panic over problems with too many variables, and skip them because I thought they just took too long to figure out. What I learned is to go through those problems and assign each person a variable and follow the instructions step by step. For me this made these types of problems so much easier.

—*Elizabeth*
  Denver, Colorado
  SAT/ACT Scores: 2100
  Claremont McKenna College

• • • • • • • •

THE MATH SECTION WAS the most challenging part for me. Not because I didn't know how to do the problems, but because I took calculus during my junior year in high school, so by that time I had forgotten all of the elementary stuff like fractions. So I bought some Princeton Review books and used them to review the materials and to refresh my memory.

—*Alice Hu*
  Redmond, Washington
  SAT/ACT Scores: 2260
  Stanford University

TOP MATH STRATEGIES

USE YOUR CALCULATOR WISELY. It's important that you know how to use your calculator before the SAT. It's also important that you realize its capabilities. Today's calculators not only do simple arithmetic functions, but also help you deal with a number of more complicated parts of the SAT Math section. Once you're certain that your model of calculator is allowed, make sure you integrate its features fully into your SAT study.

DON'T BE AFRAID TO PLUG AND CHUG. For the SAT only, forget everything you've been told about showing your work. No one's looking to test whether you remember the proper approach.

SKIP THE HARDEST PROBLEMS. Unless you think you can ace the Math section, it's important that you not spend too much time on any one question. If you run out of time, and you almost surely will, you're better off skipping the *hardest* three questions instead of the three that were randomly last in the test order.

ALLOW FOR INCREASING DIFFICULTY. The math questions generally get harder from the front to the back of each section. Don't be fooled when pacing yourself: if you're halfway done with the test after half of the time is gone, you're actually way behind, because the problems in the second half of the section will take much longer.

MATH WAS THE EASIEST SECTION for me because it covers the first two years of math in high school. But watch out: Even though it seems easy, some of the questions are really tricky. Sometimes they include in your choices two answers that could be right and you just have to choose the one that is more right which really confuses me.

—A.C.
BERKELEY, CALIFORNIA
SAT/ACT SCORES: 1800
UNIVERSITY OF CALIFORNIA, BERKELEY

• • • • • • • •

WHEN PRACTICING THE MATH SECTION, keep a list of every error you make. It may not be the most self-gratifying thing to do, but before the test you can review this list to find out which tricks commonly confuse you. I would sometimes drop my negative sign in an algebra problem, and I would also sometimes forget 0 is one of the single-digit integers. Those became the things I would look over twice when I completed those problems.

—MICHAEL WYMBS
BEACH HAVEN, NEW JERSEY
SAT/ACT SCORES: 2260

The Test: Writing Section

*M*any students think of the new SAT Writing section as simply an essay, but the essay actually makes up less than half of your Writing score. In addition to a 25-minute essay, you'll spend one 25-minute section and another 10-minute section answering multiple choice questions that test grammar, usage, and related concepts.

Unlike in Critical Reading, where students use different strategies to succeed, everyone's mostly in agreement about what makes a good SAT essay. In addition to the obvious things, like strong organization and the proper use of grammar and punctuation, you want to make sure you write plenty and that you do a good job of responding to the essay prompt with arguments and examples.

Whether you're a good writer or not, you can definitely prepare for the SAT essay by thinking in advance about your approach. Will you write a five-paragraph essay? Should you have potential examples in mind before you see the actual essay prompt? Will you try to write a lot, even if it makes your writing less concise? There aren't right answers to any of these questions: by looking at what past students did, however, you may be able to make a determination about what will work best for you.

As for the multiple-choice questions, students seem to agree that practice makes perfect. Hopefully, you'll take the advice of these former test takers and go through some practice writing questions before the SAT.

THE ESSAY IS LEARNABLE. It follows a formula. One teacher told me it's a fat sandwich on skinny bread: a really short intro, a long explanation and a conclusion. And my friend said, "As long as you use at least one semicolon, you'll be fine."

—BEN
NEW YORK, NEW YORK

* * * * * * * *

FOR THE ESSAY SECTION you are given a prompt and you pretty much have to take one side of the argument and support it in your writing. The prompt is on a topic that most people can answer. You just have to apply your writing skills, and it helps if you really focus on only one side though; be for it or against it. Use lots of examples to support your side and squeeze as much information as you can in the small space and limited amount of time you are given.

—SHARLA
KAUAI, HAWAII
SAT/ACT SCORES: 2000
🏛 UNIVERSITY OF SOUTHERN CALIFORNIA

* * * * * * * *

IN THE WRITING SECTION, the more you write, the better. Try to fill up the entire space. Use your neatest handwriting. That's the fastest way to improve your score other than writing intelligently, making a coherent argument, and using specific details from literature and history, which are also good tips. The test makers are *trying* to bore you with the Reading Comprehension part. Don't let the passages lull you to sleep! Don't try to memorize the details; instead, skim the passage, then go to the questions and refer back to the relevant part of the reading passage for the information you need. Don't get bogged down on any one passage.

—TIMOTHY MICHAEL COOPER
NEW YORK, NEW YORK
🏛 YALE UNIVERSITY

The grammar; ugh, it's so hard.

—STEFANIE LAMPRECHT
TIBURON, CALIFORNIA
SAT/ACT SCORES: 1800
🏛 SANTA CLARA UNIVERSITY

HEADLINES
Best Advice and Top Tips

- On the essay, write as much as you can. Studies have shown that longer essays grade out better.
- Take a few minutes to plan out your essay. It will help you avoid rewriting it!

TAKE A CLEAR STAND ON THE SUBJECT, even if you don't agree with it yourself. In my essay about "Is there under any circumstance a lie should ever be told?" I wrote no for some reason, but I stuck with it, and I did pretty well.

—*ANDREA PARKER*
CHICAGO, ILLINOIS
SAT/ACT SCORES: 890
SOUTHERN ILLINOIS UNIVERSITY, CARBONDALE

INSTEAD OF SIMPLE SENTENCES, mix it up by using reverse syntax, starting with participial phrases. Throw in a few ostentatious words, like "ostentatious." Put a colon in, use semicolons, cut a few dashes; they look impressive and could help boost your score.

—*JIAHAO*
SINGAPORE
SAT/ACT SCORES: 2320
MIDDLEBURY COLLEGE

DON'T OVERTHINK the Writing portion. I wanted to knock their socks off, so I spent a good 10 minutes outlining and thinking of something great to write. I had intended to write a five-paragraph essay. I got through one pretty good paragraph and then one more—and the time was up!

—*ANONYMOUS*
ST. LOUIS, MISSOURI
SAT/ACT SCORES: 2290
UNDECIDED

· · · · · · · · ·

"In the Writing sections, say everything you can about the topic. Tests have shown that they look for length as well as a solid argument. "

—*COLLEEN DAVIS*
LEXINGTON, KENTUCKY
SAT/ACT SCORES: 2150/31
WASHINGTON UNIVERSITY IN ST. LOUIS

· · · · · · · · ·

I TOOK AS MANY PRACTICE TESTS as I could and I tried to find similarities between them. I noticed, for example, that a lot of them were written in a quasi-narrative form, just talking about an experience that made the writer have the opinion that they do. So I basically used that form. I answered the prompt by explaining how one day convinced me of a certain idea. And no, I didn't lay out three historical, personal, and literary examples.

—*ANONYMOUS*
MIAMI, FLORIDA
SAT/ACT SCORES: 2320
COLUMBIA UNIVERSITY

Write as much as you possibly can. That seems to be what the graders care about.

—ANONYMOUS
ST. LOUIS,
MISSOURI
WILLIAMS COLLEGE

I'M AN ENGLISH AS A Second Language student. The essays were a problem. When I took my first SAT, I had to make the outline in Korean (because I thought in Korean a lot faster than I thought in English) and then translate into English, and then fill in the rest. So in the first SAT I did not have the time to finish the essay, and for the first few practice tests I never seemed to finish the essay on time. This is where I got outside help from friends who have taken the class. They told me to use the simple five-paragraph format, with an introduction, body paragraphs, and endings. The reason I was not so sure about using this format in the first place was that I heard that too many people were using this format, and unless you write really elegantly, it was hard to get a good score. I actually don't know why I believed in that but I changed my perspective. As I got better with English, I was able to gradually think better in English, write up the five-paragraph outline, and write the essay on time.

—JIKYU CHOI
FAIR OAKS, CALIFORNIA
SAT/ACT SCORES: 2370
STANFORD UNIVERSITY

• • • • • • • •

ON THE ESSAY, you should think of three to six examples that could be stretched and used as support for subjects that you don't know much about. Mine were The Holocaust, The Beat Generation of the 1950s, The War on Iraq, the Darfur Crisis, *The Catcher in the Rye*, and *Macbeth*. I didn't end up using any of them because I was able to think of a more appropriate example based on the question.

—CHRIS DELGROSSO
MOORESTOWN, NEW JERSEY
SAT/ACT SCORES: 2050
EMERSON COLLEGE

SAT HORROR STORY #72

My friend once wrote an entire SAT essay on being Jewish because he thought the essay question was asking about ethnics, not ethics.

—*ELIZABETH*
MADISON, WISCONSIN
SAT/ACT SCORES: 1260/28
UNIVERSITY OF SOUTHERN CALIFORNIA

THE ESSAY QUESTIONS ARE really broad and general. They are going to ask you things like: Is creativity important? Is being courageous important? Do you need to have good leadership skills to be successful? The best way to answer these types of questions is to write about someone famous from history, like Martin Luther King. Almost anyone in history could fit into an answer. And since you don't have to write that much, you should only familiarize yourself with a few historical leaders at the basic level. I would get children's books from the library and read those, and you'll have enough information to get you through the essay. Remember, English teachers are grading your essay, so they are going to be impressed that you know about someone from history. The children's books are so short and to the point and that's all you need to know. You could also go on a website that summarizes books for you.

—*LINDSAY*
LOS ANGELES, CALIFORNIA
SAT/ACT SCORES: 1760
UNIVERSITY OF CALIFORNIA, SANTA BARBARA

WHAT'S TESTED IN THE SAT WRITING SECTION?

A writing section is new to the SAT as of 2005: it is why the total number of points that can be earned on the SAT increased from 1600 to 2400. Essentially, the College Board added what was previously the SAT II Writing test (required by many top colleges) to the existing SAT. While some changes were made to the Math and Critical Reading sections of the test, the biggest change by far was the introduction of the Writing section—and with it, the essay.

According to the College Board, the SAT Writing section tests "grammar, usage, and word choice." While a timed essay is part of the section (25 of the 60 minutes), there are also three different types of multiple-choice questions.

Essay graders grade each essay on a 1-6 scale and are looking for the things that traditionally make a good essay: organization, grammar and usage, transitions, use of examples, etc.

The other three SAT Writing question types are all multiple choice. These test your understanding of basic grammar and usage principles, including everything from verb tenses to sentence order. Students are presented with a writing portion and asked either to improve it or to point out where it contains an error.

I TOOK THE **PSAT** with no prep at all, just to see what I would get, and I got a 230, which is comparable to getting a 2300 on the SAT. I felt that I did not need to prepare for the SAT. But the PSAT doesn't have an essay, and my Writing score ended up dropping 70 points because I didn't really prepare for the essay enough. Practice writing essays in 20 minutes, and have general "fallback topics" in mind ahead of time. The essay prompt will generally ask for examples— literary, historical or personal—to help prove your point. For me, having made a list of four or five books that I had read recently would have helped me a lot, because you get in there and your mind freezes.

—*BECKY*
NEWTON, MASSACHUSETTS
SAT/ACT SCORES: 2290
SWARTHMORE COLLEGE

. . . .

" Use your transition words, like 'finally,' 'furthermore,' 'next,' 'moreover,' and 'in conclusion' in your essays to make the judges know that you know how to go from one point to the next. "

—*ANDREA PARKER*
CHICAGO, ILLINOIS
SAT/ACT SCORES: 890
SOUTHERN ILLINOIS UNIVERSITY, CARBONDALE

Make sure you know what you're going to write about before you start. You don't have enough time to start over.

—*David*
St. Louis, Missouri
SAT/ACT Scores: 2020/29
University of Wisconsin

THE WRITING IS THE EASIEST SECTION, so people tend to blow off studying for it. You don't have to do much since most of it is grammar and rules from the 5th grade. Just brush up on some novels you've read and some current events. You need specific examples for the essay and you really need to fill both pages to get an 11 or 12. I just browsed through some topics of books I had read throughout the year and I applied knowledge from American history classes and current events. You can also use personal experiences, or you can even make up personal experiences if you wish. Take advantage of this section; a good score on it can only help.

—*Tom O'Brien*
Scranton, Pennsylvania
SAT/ACT Scores: 2160
Undecided

• • • • • • • •

BEFORE READING THE ESSAY PROMPT, it helps to have a skeletal outline in mind; in addition to writing an introduction and a conclusion, I planned to support my thesis with three paragraphs: one discussing a novel, another a historical event, and a third a current event. I had a couple of books, historical events, and current events in mind that I thought I could easily adapt to whatever topic was given.

—*Brooke*
St. Louis, Missouri
Princeton University

• • • • • • • •

THEY GIVE YOU A SINGLE PAGE of writing so it's not even an essay; it's about how tight you can squeeze your words and how many cool facts you can throw out there. Remember that the reader is only going to look at your essay for a minute or less.

—*Aaron*
Beverly Hills, California
SAT/ACT Scores: 2150
University of California, Berkeley

I RETOOK THE **SAT** IN **JUNE,** after learning my spring results were lower than those of my sophomore year. This time I wasted no time on overplanning the essay. I just wrote, using a mental outline that held together well, I think. I felt I had written all I could on the topic. I followed the advice and wrote more neatly than before.

—*HARRISON S. BAER*
MOORHEAD, MINNESOTA

"No matter what you do, don't go off topic on the essay. The length doesn't matter; the test scorers just want to see that you can focus on one idea and see it through to the end of the essay. "

—*CHRISTIE*
CINCINNATI, OHIO
SAT/ACT SCORES: 2120
UNIVERSITY OF CHARLESTON

MAKE THE ESSAY VERY SHORT and concise and don't try to write anything amazing. I wrote about the necessity of perseverance and dedication to success. I tried to find a historical example, a literary example and a personal example. The books say you should do that, and it worked pretty well for me.

—*ALEXANDER*
PROVIDENCE, RHODE ISLAND
BROWN UNIVERSITY

TOP WRITING SECTION STRATEGIES

WRITE A LONG ESSAY. Investigations have shown, and common sense dictates, that human essay graders tend to assume students are better writers when they write long essays.

PLAN YOUR ESSAY. If you spend three to four minutes planning your essay before beginning to write, you'll do a much better job keeping it organized, integrating examples, and knowing what you want to write about.

IDENTIFY THE SPECIFIC MISTAKE IN MULTIPLE-CHOICE QUESTIONS. It's crucial that you don't just answer these questions by determining which selection "sounds" or "feels" right. Almost always there will be something that's objectively, definitively wrong about a wrong answer choice. Try to find the problem, rather than just relying on your instincts.

CHECK ALL OF THE ANSWERS. Answer C may sound good until you take a good look at D. If you have time, look at every answer choice before you choose one.

Apples & Oranges: Differences in the SAT & ACT

W*hile the SAT is the dominant college admissions exam on the coasts, the ACT is popular in the Midwest and the South. Almost as many students take the ACT as take the SAT, and the test has received a great deal of attention lately as an alternative to the SAT. Many colleges allow students to submit scores from either test. You should check with each college to which you're applying to find out which test(s) they accept.*

So, how is the ACT different from the SAT? The differences between the two tests are probably overstated, and the introduction of the "new" SAT in 2005 probably made the tests even more alike. Sure, they're scored differently and have different question types. And the ACT has a science section and makes the essay optional. But generally, these two exams test the same things: writing skills, reading comprehension, math knowledge, etc.

In our experience, there's probably a little bit of truth to the general perception that the ACT is a little more of a substantive test, while the SAT focuses more on ability and reasoning skills. ACT math questions seem to cover a more broad and deep cross-section of the high school math curriculum, whereas SAT math questions are hard but may rely more on math ability than actual knowledge of advanced concepts. The SAT essay questions almost always seem more complicated and thus more concerned with analysis than the more straightforward ACT essay questions. No vocabulary is tested on the ACT, which benefits the average high school student who hasn't read extensively or studied vocabulary outside of school.

Read on to find out what other students thought about the ACT and how it compares to the SAT.

I THOUGHT THE **ACT** was easier than the SAT, especially the Writing section. The only negatives on the ACT were the Science section and the time factor. The Science section was something I had never seen and I wasn't prepared. I also didn't finish the test on time because the ACT has a lot more questions on it than the SAT. I should've studied for it a little more but couldn't because I was pressed for time. Even without studying though, I still did well overall.

—ELIZABETH
DENVER, COLORADO
SAT/ACT SCORES: 2100
CLAREMONT MCKENNA COLLEGE

• • • • • • • •

" Be familiar with the ACT directions before you take the test. One of my very intelligent friends ended up making a 23 because she spent half the time trying to understand the directions in the English section. "

—N.R.
MEMPHIS, TENNESSEE
SAT/ACT SCORES: 1260/35
UNDECIDED

• • • • • • • • •

GOOD AT SCIENCE? Take the ACT. Not so good at science? Skip it.

—ELIZABETH
MADISON, WISCONSIN
SAT/ACT SCORES: 1260/28
UNIVERSITY OF SOUTHERN CALIFORNIA

On the ACT, the Science section tests more of your speed-reading and compre-hension skills rather than actual science knowledge.

—BEN
  SPRINGFIELD,
  ILLINOIS
  SAT/ACT
  SCORES: 2200/32
  🏛 UNIVERSITY OF
  ILLINOIS, URBANA-
  CHAMPAIGN

I PREFER THE SAT. Although everyone hates having 10 sections, I actually prefer those 25-minute sections to the ACT's immensely long sections. The Math section on the ACT is, I think, 60 minutes long. By the last 10 minutes, my back was hurting and my eyes were straining. But what are worse are the Reading and Science sections, not because they are too long; the difficulty is in trying to finish. If you read everything, there's no way to finish, so you have to skim; but by skimming you risk losing information. It's just a pain.

—N.R.
  MEMPHIS, TENNESSEE
  SAT/ACT SCORES: 1260/35
  🏛 UNDECIDED

• • • • • • • •

TAKE BOTH TESTS. I think that colleges like to see the SAT because it has been around for so long that they feel it is a good benchmark. But how you do depends on the type of person you are, so why not take both? The best thing about the ACT is that if you do poorly on it, you don't have to send your scores.

—VIDYA SATHYAMOORTHY
  ROCKVILLE, MARYLAND
  SAT/ACT SCORES: 2160/33
  🏛 UNDECIDED

• • • • • • • •

I THINK THE ACT IS BETTER than the SAT for people who aren't as good at math and reasoning. I took both tests and I felt the ACT was really testing my knowledge, like the things I was learning about in school, whereas the SAT was more abstract and more about testing reasoning and critical-thinking skills.

—LAURA
  CINCINNATI, OHIO
  SAT/ACT SCORES: 31
  🏛 FRANCISCAN UNIVERSITY OF STEUBENVILLE

I PREFER THE **SAT** TO THE **ACT,** except for their crappy essays. Their essays are so bland and dead that I feel I cannot express my individuality. Plus, the ACT has it structured so that you take four large bulky tests, each on the same topic, whereas the SAT alternates math, reading and writing so that things are not so tedious and you do not find yourself dozing off. Despite this, I would suggest taking both because some people excel on one over the other.

—*JAKE M. KENNEDY*
HICKORY HILLS, ILLINOIS
SAT/ACT SCORES: 2100/33
UNIVERSITY OF SOUTHERN CALIFORNIA

My SAT scores translated to a 31 on the ACT, and when I took the ACT I got a 32, which was a definite improvement.

—*BURTON DEWITT*
MELVILLE,
NEW YORK
SAT/ACT
SCORES: 2080/32
RICE
UNIVERSITY

· · · · · · · · ·

WITH THE ACT, I rocked the Science section my first time taking it, and the second time I didn't do so well. Make sure that you know how to arrange data from experiments. And I stress this: physics! I am not a physics person, which cost me the second time I took the test. Look over basic physics equations and terms.

—*RYAN BATES*
HUDSON, WISCONSIN

ACT INFO

The national average ACT composite score for 2006: 21.1, an increase from 20.9 in 2005.

Number of students that took the test: More than 1.2 million

The highest possible ACT score: 36

How many 2006 test-takers scored 36: About 1 in 5,500

PROS AND CONS

There are a few distinctive characteristics of the ACT. First, there are four sections: English, Reading, Math and Science. There is no Science section on the SAT. Also, you take each section continuously, whereas on the SAT they are broken up into smaller sections of 20-30 minutes that appear intermittently. Also, for the ACT your score is reported with subscores, so it shows your strength in certain subtopics. For instance, if you are better at algebra than trigonometry, it will be represented in your subscore. These details give a better perception of the person as a whole.

The only negative aspect of the ACT in my eyes was in the Science section. I am generally strong at science, but I consistently did worse on the Science section than I would have expected. I think that time may have been a factor in this, as well as the format of the section. You are given tables, graphs and excerpts of an experiment, and then asked a series of questions on them. This format makes it difficult to comprehend the experiment as a whole. Also, in order to finish the section within the time limit, you can't skim the information before looking at the questions. The more effective way is to start with the questions and refer back to the tables and charts. I think that this detracts from your overall ability to answer the questions.

—*VIDYA SATHYAMOORTHY*
ROCKVILLE, MARYLAND
SAT/ACT SCORES: 2160/33
UNDECIDED

I WAS SURPRISED TO FIND THAT the Science section on the ACT had absolutely nothing to do with the science or chemistry or biology that I had been learning in school. It's more about proficiencies and reasoning than actual scientific content. Don't think that just because you do well in those subjects you'll do fine on the test—you should still take some practice tests so you get a feel for what it's about.

—*TEKLA TOMAN*
YOUNGSTOWN, OHIO
SAT/ACT SCORES: 29
XAVIER UNIVERSITY

THE REASON I THINK THE ACT is more straightforward is because an SAT question may ask a question like "Which one best emphasizes …?" On the ACT, that would be phrased as "Which statement makes the most grammatical sense?" One is definitive while the other is more opinioned. I would always recommend the ACT because I think the questions are easier to understand.

—*ANDREW*
MEQUON, WISCONSIN
SAT/ACT SCORES: 2210/35
DUKE UNIVERSITY

The ACT is an achievement test and the SAT is an aptitude test. The ACT tests you on what you know instead of what you could know.

—*BURTON DEWITT*
MELVILLE,
NEW YORK
SAT/ACT
SCORES: 2080/32
RICE
UNIVERSITY

I THINK EVERYONE should at least practice each test so they can see which one fits them better. I preferred the SAT over the ACT, because I felt that breaking it up into a lot of sections made it less overwhelming, and I did not feel as rushed for time. If I had to do it all over again, I would not take the ACT, because the SAT seemed to fit my test-taking abilities better, seeing as I felt that enough time was given for the sections.

—*BEN*
SPRINGFIELD, ILLINOIS
SAT/ACT SCORES: 2200/32
UNIVERSITY OF ILLINOIS, URBANA-CHAMPAIGN

HEAD TO HEAD: SAT VS. ACT

While the SAT and ACT generally test the same concepts, these are definitely two different tests. The key differences:

	SAT	ACT
Math	Arithmetic, algebra, and geometry. Problems are more unusual and can occasionally feel like IQ test questions.	Math is more advanced (and includes some trigonometry), but questions are usually more straightforward.
Writing/English	Three types of multiple choice questions that test grammar and usage. Subject-verb agreement, present vs. past tense, etc.	Lots of punctuation including commas, semicolons, etc. Also grammar and various writing issues.
Reading Comprehension	Passages are different lengths.	Passages are roughly the same length.
Science	No science questions.	Science passages that test reasoning, not actual science knowledge.
Essay	Mandatory 25-minute essay folded into the Writing score. Questions can be abstract and difficult.	Optional 30-minute essay usually asks a simple question about school policy.

	SAT	ACT
Vocabulary	Sentence completion questions test vocabulary somewhat—still, it's nothing like what used to be on the SAT.	Vocabulary not tested.
Time/Format	10 sections (one experimental). 3 hours and 45 minutes.	4 sections plus optional essay. 2 hours and 55 minutes (or 3:25 with essay).
Scoring	600- 2400. Three scores from 200-800 are added together. The essay is folded into the Writing score.	1-36. Four scores from 1-36 are averaged together. The essay is optional and is thus scored separately.
Guessing	There is a penalty for wrong answers. Typically, guessing will leave you with the same average score (but with a higher variance) than leaving a bubble blank.	No penalty for guessing means you should always answer every question.

THE SCIENCE SECTION on the ACT is the analysis of graphs and reports. The questions include predicting events, analyzing data/graphs, and comparing lab reports. This came naturally to me but many people report having a problem with this section. Stay calm on the ACT Science section. At first, the problems look complex and challenging but after two read-throughs of the data and reports, the questions are very straightforward.

—*ANDREW*
MEQUON, WISCONSIN
SAT/ACT SCORES: 2210/35
DUKE UNIVERSITY

● ● ● ● ● ● ● ● ●

THE ACT READING SECTION is more straightforward than the SAT Reading section, but it is way more rushed. On the ACT you get 35 minutes to answer 40 questions and on the SAT you have 25 minutes to answer about 20 questions. Also, about five of those 20 questions are quickly answered.

—*ANONYMOUS*
ORANGE, CALIFORNIA
SAT/ACT SCORES: 2190/33
UNDECIDED

TEST TIME

The ACT takes a little over four hours, without the Writing Test, including administration instructions and breaks. Actual testing time is 2 hours and 55 minutes, broken down as follows:

English: 45 minutes
Math: 60 minutes
Reading: 35 minutes
Science: 35 minutes

The ACT Writing Test adds 30 minutes to the testing time.

Your No. 2 Pencil and ___? Last-Minute Preparations

*T*est day is finally here. If you've done your preparation, the last things you should be worried about by the time Saturday morning rolls around are math formulas, grammar rules, and vocabulary words. You probably shouldn't even be thinking about that stuff the day before the SAT. Would a marathon runner do a lot of running the day before the big race, or warm up with a quick 5K? You need to be fresh for the test, and that means letting your mind relax.

Your mind and body function together, and being comfortable physically is essential if you want your brain to stay focused.

Comfortable clothes (layers are best), a good breakfast (we recommend some protein), and caffeine (if you're used to it) are all recommended by past test-takers.

What do you need to bring? Have you checked the batteries in your calculator lately? Did you get a good night's sleep? What about on Thursday night? Do you trust your alarm clock? How are you going to get to the test center? Does the driver know the way to go?

For tips on these questions and more, read on.

KNOW WHEN THE SAT TAKES PLACE! I forgot about my SATs! I was not motivated at all to take it since I was already content with my ACT score and was confident that I would not do any worse than I had on the PSAT. So one night I came home at 1 a.m. and saw my SAT registration paper on the table, and I realized I had to wake up in five hours to take it. I got to sleep ASAP, and when the alarm went off I wanted to go back to bed.

> —ANDREW
> MEQUON, WISCONSIN
> SAT/ACT SCORES: 2210/35
> DUKE UNIVERSITY

• • • • • • • •

FOR ME THE BEST THING I did to calm my nerves before taking the SAT was to avoid sugar and caffeine for 24 hours before the test until after the test was over. The first two times I took the test I was very jumpy. I thought eating candy and drinking coffee would help me stay awake, but it just stressed me out and made me nervous. I tried taking it the final time without anything, and I was totally relaxed.

> —M.C.
> KALAMAZOO, MICHIGAN
> SAT/ACT SCORES: 2260/33
> UNDECIDED

• • • • • • • •

I WOKE UP ON THE MORNING of the SAT and ate a good breakfast to give my brain some food to function. I went over the notes that I had been studying for the previous weeks. Then, I made sure my calculator had batteries and that I was at the test site 20 minutes before the test started to make sure that I did not miss it.

> —BRITTANY ELYSE GRAHAM
> WEST CHESTER, PENNSYLVANIA
> SAT/ACT SCORES: 890/21
> INDIANA UNIVERSITY OF PENNSYLVANIA

I kept myself from getting stressed out before and during the test by taking the advice from my parents to just leave it in God's hands.

> —BRITTANY
> MCCOMBS
> VENICE, CALIFORNIA
> SAT/ACT
> SCORES: 1000
> SYRACUSE
> UNIVERSITY

HEADLINES
Best Advice and Top Tips

- Get a good night's sleep for several nights before the test. Eat a good breakfast on the morning of the test.
- Have everything you need—including calculator and directions to the testing site—laid out the night before.
- Leave plenty of time to travel to the testing site.

Give yourself plenty of time to get there in the morning.

—*Tori*
Birmingham, Alabama
SAT/ACT Scores: 2300/34

My dad told me to eat a chocolate bar about 20 minutes before taking the test, because chocolate releases endorphins in your system and helps your brain react quicker. I'm not sure if it's true, but it gave me a good excuse to eat a bar of chocolate at nine in the morning!

—*Jennifer Stewart*
Murfreesboro, Tennessee
SAT/ACT Scores: 25
Middle Tennessee State University

• • • • • • • • •

A librarian told me the day before the exam to just read something enjoyable that night and don't study, but be sure to get a good night's sleep and eat something with Omega-3 fatty acid, like salmon or tuna. I don't know how much good that Omega-3 did in reality, but it definitely got me thinking I was ready mentally.

—*Ronald Jordan Hinson*
Lenoir, North Carolina
SAT/ACT Scores: 1940
Clemson University

ON THE DAY OF YOUR TEST, trick your body into thinking it is afternoon, not morning. I don't always agree with the morning, so I went to bed earlier and woke up earlier, read the paper and went out for breakfast. They say your "biological clock" feels like it's later in the day.

> —*TOM O'BRIEN*
> *SCRANTON, PENNSYLVANIA*
> *SAT/ACT SCORES: 2160*
> *UNDECIDED*

. . . .

" The most important thing to remember—and this is not a joke—is to visit the bathroom before the test starts. It sounds obvious, but a lot of people forget. You'll be glad you did! "

> —*S.M.*
> *MAHWAH, NEW JERSEY*
> *SAT/ACT SCORES: 1310*
> *PENNSYLVANIA STATE UNIVERSITY*

. . . .

RIDE WITH A PARENT if you have to take the test at a location other than your own high school. I had a horrible experience finding the testing center, and when I got there the front gate was locked and I had to try and find the back entrance through a neighborhood. The drive caused a lot of stress, which is the last thing anyone needs before the SAT. If you ride with a parent you don't have to worry about whether you'll be able to find the place, or if there will be enough parking available.

> —*PHILLIP LAVIN*
> *MARIETTA, GEORGIA*

Check Google Maps before you leave your house.

—*MIKE MELLENTHIN*
MENLO PARK,
CALIFORNIA
SAT/ACT
SCORES: 2340
STANFORD
UNIVERSITY

I OVERSLEPT THE FIRST TIME I was supposed to take the SAT, and I missed it entirely. It was my best friend's birthday the night before and I ended up staying out with her until four in the morning. My parents were so mad at me, but fortunately it was early in my junior year and I had plenty of time to take it again later.

—*MOLLY*
LAS VEGAS, NEVADA
UNIVERSITY OF ARIZONA

• • • • • • • •

I HAD MY MOTHER GIVE ME a ride to the test. I didn't know exactly where to go and that way I didn't have to worry about getting lost.

—*ANONYMOUS*
ST. LOUIS, MISSOURI
SAT/ACT SCORES: 2290
UNDECIDED

• • • • • • • •

WAKE UP A LITTLE EARLIER THAN USUAL; it will calm your nerves if you can move at a slower pace in the morning. I know a few of my class-mates have overslept for the SAT. Luckily they still had plenty of time to take the test before sending out college applications, but they still lost the registration money.

—*PHILLIP LAVIN*
MARIETTA, GEORGIA

• • • • • • • •

BRING A SOMEWHAT HEALTHY SNACK to the test. I was starving by the time we had our break, and I was so glad to have it. It helped me gain back a little energy for the rest of the test—something I doubt the old chocolate bars in the vending machines did for other test-takers.

—*TEKLA TOMAN*
YOUNGSTOWN, OHIO
SAT/ACT SCORES: 29
XAVIER UNIVERSITY

SAT HORROR STORY #201

The first time I signed up to take my SAT was the morning after a big high school football game. I planned on going home right after the game, but all of my friends were going out to celebrate our school's victory and I couldn't say no. I ended up getting pretty drunk and in the morning I was so hung over that I just stayed in bed and slept through the test. There was absolutely no way I was going to get up and sit in a room for over four hours.

—BRYAN
LAS VEGAS, NEVADA
SAT/ACT SCORES: 2110
UNIVERSITY OF SOUTHERN CALIFORNIA

IF YOU TAKE THE TEST ANY TIME other than summer, make sure you take a jacket or sweater. A lot of schools turn off their heat over the weekend, which is when the test takes place. At one of my test-taking sessions, they forgot to leave it on for the test, and I froze the whole time!

—JOHN STEPHEN REBER
CINCINNATI, OHIO
SAT/ACT SCORES: 2200
GEORGETOWN UNIVERSITY

• • • • • • • •

THE DAY BEFORE THE EXAM I did not study, I didn't talk about it with my family, and I didn't daydream about it. Instead I engaged in high impact aerobics, and went to bed early. I then got up early the next day because the test was not administered at my school, and I had to give myself enough time to find the school on the other side of town.

—TSHINO KANKWENDA
MONTREAL, CANADA

Turn off your phone—they *will* take your test if it rings!

—COLLEEN DAVIS
LEXINGTON, KENTUCKY
SAT/ACT SCORES: 2150/31
WASHINGTON UNIVERSITY IN ST. LOUIS

MIND OVER MATTER IN YOUR STOMACH

TRY TO AVOID EATING TOO MUCH BEFORE THE TEST. Obviously you need some type of nourishment in order to think at the highest level possible, but too much food and a nervous stomach can result in discomfort during the test. If you start to feel sick during the test you'll lose focus and have a very hard time scoring well on it.

—*PHILLIP LAVIN*
MARIETTA, GEORGIA

DON'T EAT A HUGE BREAKFAST BEFORE YOU TAKE THE SAT. I had too much to eat, and as soon as I sat down I felt an overwhelming urge to go to sleep. It wasn't the best way to start the test and it totally affected my score. The second time I took it, my scores went up over 200 points. That much of an increase is so rare, so I can only guess that it had to do with being too full and too sleepy.

—*CODY*
PHOENIX, ARIZONA
SAT/ACT SCORES: 1900
UNIVERSITY OF ARIZONA

AVOID COFFEE. INSTEAD, DRINK WATER OR JUICE; it is calming to the stomach. Also, because people "doctor" their coffee, all of the sugar is running through their bodies.

—*CASEY PONTIOUS*
LOCUST GROVE, OKLAHOMA
FREE WILL BAPTIST BIBLE COLLEGE

ON THE MORNING OF THE TEST, I drank purple grape juice. There was an article in the newspaper about a couple of kids who both made perfect scores on the old SAT and they said they drank grape juice in the morning.

—*ALEX*
BIRMINGHAM, ALABAMA
SAT/ACT SCORES: 2350/36

I WISH I BROUGHT MORE FOOD TO THE EXAM. I was so hungry and all I had was a granola bar. I had to get up so early to get to the testing center, too early to even eat breakfast, but once I got there I was hungry.

>—*LIVIA ROMANO*
>*SAN DIEGO, CALIFORNIA*
>*SAT/ACT SCORES: 2020*
>*CLAREMONT MCKENNA COLLEGE*

I DRANK COFFEE AND I WAS FINE FOR THE FIRST SECTION and then I crashed. I hit that caffeine low, which is something you definitely don't want to do when you have four hours of rigorous test work ahead of you.

>—*BRADLEY HOUSTON*
>*AUSTIN, TEXAS*
>*SAT/ACT SCORES: 2050/32*
>*RICE UNIVERSITY*

BEFORE THE TEST, I ATE SOME PEPPERMINTS. My mom said they're supposed to sharpen your thinking and make you more aware. But all I know for sure is that they taste good.

>—*ANONYMOUS*
>*SEATTLE, WASHINGTON*

I MADE SURE TO FINISH all of my reviewing and practicing two days before I actually took the test so that I could feel confident and ready. The day before the test I didn't concentrate on having to take the test the next day and chose to relax. I also made sure that I laid out my admission ticket, pencils, calculator, snack and all other materials the night before so I wouldn't be in a rush to find them in the morning.

—*Terrahney Wilson*
Lithonia, Georgia
SAT/ACT Scores: 1950
UNDECIDED

" Make plans with your friends to do something fun immediately following the exam, and the whole experience will be more enjoyable. "

—*Graham Lederer*
Brookeville, Maryland
SAT/ACT Scores: 1470
College of William and Mary

I DIDN'T LEAVE MYSELF enough time from waking up to getting to the testing center. It was a few factors: traffic; finding the actual center; making breakfast; just poor planning in general. I also didn't have a very big breakfast the day of the test, and I wasn't comfortable. I just didn't feel ready. All the little things the night and morning before the test do make a difference.

—*Peter William Finnocchiaro*
Baldwinsville, New York
SAT/ACT Scores: 2300/32
UNDECIDED

THE MORNING I TOOK MY SAT I overslept and then when I got in my car learned that they closed the freeway entrance by my house. I was about ten minutes late for the exam so I ran into the room, interrupted everyone and started the test.

—*MIKE MELLENTHIN*
MENLO PARK, CALIFORNIA
SAT/ACT SCORES: 2340
STANFORD UNIVERSITY

Forget cramming. Get some sleep.

—*JAWON LEE*
SAN DIEGO, CALIFORNIA
SAT/ACT SCORES: 2400

GET A GOOD NIGHT'S SLEEP. I actually fell asleep for five minutes during the SAT! I still answered all the questions and did well, but if you need the full allotted time, falling asleep would definitely be a problem.

—*B.A.R.*
HILTON HEAD, SOUTH CAROLINA
SAT/ACT SCORES: 1480
WASHINGTON UNIVERSITY IN ST. LOUIS

DON'T DRINK COFFEE BEFORE THE SAT. I had the worst stomachache and really had to go to the bathroom. It was so bad that I couldn't concentrate on an entire section of the test. If you really need coffee to start your day, get up 30 minutes earlier so you can drink it at home.

—*BRYAN*
LAS VEGAS, NEVADA
SAT/ACT SCORES: 2110
UNIVERSITY OF SOUTHERN CALIFORNIA

DO NOT FORGET YOUR CALCULATOR! I forgot mine in my locker and my teacher would not let me go get it. I cried to him and he still wouldn't let me go. Needless to say, I did not do well on the Math section, especially considering math is my worst subject.

—*ALEXXA CONDON*
CHANNAHON, ILLINOIS
SOUTHERN ILLINOIS UNIVERSITY, CARBONDALE

WEAR A WATCH. The worst feeling in the world is getting into the room and realizing you can't see the clock from your assigned seat! Especially when the proctors won't tell you what time it is. But make sure your watch doesn't have an alarm that goes off every hour, because then you will get kicked out, or at least get mean stares from everyone around you for the next three hours.

—*GENEVIEVE OTTO*
ST. LOUIS, MISSOURI
SAT/ACT SCORES: 2030
WASHINGTON UNIVERSITY IN ST. LOUIS

"I went to bed really early the night before my SAT and made a pact with myself to not study or read anything at all. It is really important to give your brain a break."

—*CESAR OCAMPO*
MONTEREY PARK, CALIFORNIA

YOU NEED TO MAKE SURE you follow the ID instructions they give you. I had a school ID with me and not my driver's license. Luckily a bunch of my classmates were there and they vouched for me, but really they should have sent me home.

—*ANDREW TIMBERLAKE*
BIRMINGHAM, ALABAMA
SAT/ACT SCORES: 2400
YALE UNIVERSITY

A GOOD NIGHT'S SLEEP

IT'S REALLY IMPORTANT TO GET A FULL NIGHT'S SLEEP the night before your test, but don't try to go to bed too much earlier than you are used to because your internal clock will be completely off and it will really mess you up. I usually go to bed at midnight, but decided to go to bed at ten the night before my SAT, and I woke up feeling more tired than ever.

—*A.C.*
BERKELEY, CALIFORNIA
SAT/ACT SCORES: 1800
UNIVERSITY OF CALIFORNIA, BERKELEY

• • • • • • • •

IT'S NOT JUST IMPORTANT TO GET A GOOD NIGHT'S SLEEP the night before the exam; you need to be in the habit of being well rested several days before the test. I usually go to bed really late, so starting two weeks before my scheduled date, I started going to bed an hour earlier than usual each night. If I didn't do that, I would have never been able to go to bed at a reasonable hour and I would've been so tired the morning of my exam.

—*ASHLEY*
SAN FRANCISCO, CALIFORNIA
SAT/ACT SCORES: 2100
UNIVERSITY OF SOUTHERN CALIFORNIA

Wear something that you'll be comfortable in for a few hours, but not sweats or pajamas; doing that will make you want to go to sleep.

—*CASEY PONTIOUS*
LOCUST GROVE,
OKLAHOMA
FREE WILL
BAPTIST BIBLE
COLLEGE

KEEP YOUR EYE ON THE PRIZE but don't get too stressed about it all. When you take the SATs, don't think, "OMG!!! IF I DO BADLY, I WILL NOT GET INTO COLLEGE!!!!" That approach will make you do worse.

—*DAVID*
SYOSSET, NEW YORK
SAT/ACT SCORES: 2270
DUKE UNIVERSITY

• • • • • • • •

ON THE MORNING OF THE TEST, be sure to eat a big, healthy breakfast. Both of these things can improve your concentration during the test and ease some of your nervousness.

—*ASHLEY WILLIAMS*
MEADVILLE, PENNSYLVANIA
SAT/ACT SCORES: 780
INDIANA UNIVERSITY OF PENNSYLVANIA

• • • • • • • •

EVERYONE TALKS ABOUT EATING a good breakfast, but don't forget to dress comfortably, too. Dress in layers so you can adjust to the temperature in the room. It's not a fashion show; it's a long, grueling test. You should put your comfort before everything else.

—*CHRISTIE*
CINCINNATI, OHIO
SAT/ACT SCORES: 2120
UNIVERSITY OF CHARLESTON

• • • • • • • •

PACK YOUR STUFF THE NIGHT before the exam and make sure you have all the required identification. There is nothing worse than showing up for the test after all the time you spent studying only to find out that you can't actually take the test because you don't have the right materials or identification.

—*ELIZABETH*
MADISON, WISCONSIN
SAT/ACT SCORES: 1260/28
UNIVERSITY OF SOUTHERN CALIFORNIA

OVERPREPARATION CAN LEAD you to forget the most basic essentials. When I took the SAT II Math test I forgot my calculator. I was on the way to a distant test center, went back home to pick it up, and ended up showing up 30 minutes late. Fortunately the school was a mess and they started testing 30 minutes after I arrived.

> —NIKITA BIER
> PALOS VERDES, CALIFORNIA
> SAT/ACT SCORES: 2100
> STANFORD UNIVERSITY

• • • • • • • •

ALWAYS HAVE A CHECKLIST of what to bring, or have all of your papers set out the night before the test. During spring of our junior year, one of my less conscientious friends and I were scheduled to take the SAT on the same day in a neighboring town. I picked him up, and we drove over to the school with enough time to park, sign in and settle ourselves, but no more. As we were walking in the door, he realized that he had forgotten to bring any form of ID with him, and he wanted me to drive him home to get it. He was able to talk to the test administrators, who phoned our high school and confirmed his identity, but we could easily have both missed the test.

> —SANDI BRYNN CONROY
> HADDON TOWNSHIP, NEW JERSEY
> SAT/ACT SCORES: 1440
> PENNSYLVANIA STATE UNIVERSITY

• • • • • • • •

BRING SEVERAL PENCILS. I even brought my own sharpener, which was a good thing because the room had no sharpener and everyone was using mine! Some people brought their own clocks, or pillows—whatever is comforting and makes you feel secure.

> —MICHAL ROSENOER
> CORTE MADERA, CALIFORNIA
> SAT/ACT SCORES: 2220
> UNIVERSITY OF CALIFORNIA, BERKELEY

I just made sure I got a lot of sleep the night before and I decided not to worry about it.

> —HOLLY
> HOLT, MICHIGAN
> SAT/ACT
> SCORES: 2070/34
> WASHINGTON
> UNIVERSITY IN ST.
> LOUIS

Consider

TEST + REGULATION CALCULATOR = GOOD!

MAKE SURE YOUR CALCULATOR IS REGULATION. They have special rules about what kind of calculator you can use. Some calculators can do things without you having to do any math; you're not allowed to use those. You're also not allowed to use ones with keyboards or ones that can communicate.

> —*HAYLEY*
> *LA CROSSE, WISCONSIN*
> *SAT/ACT SCORES: 34*
> *YALE UNIVERSITY*

* * * * * * * *

BRING EXTRA BATTERIES TO THE EXAM AND IF YOU CAN, an extra calculator. My calculator died during the exam, so I winged it. I called the instructor over to see if I could get batteries or a calculator, but I couldn't. Sometimes they will help you, but I've learned that if you have a mean instructor they won't give you batteries or another calculator; I had one of those mean instructors.

> —*RAYNA*
> *NEEDHAM, MASSACHUSETTS*
> *SAT/ACT SCORES: 2280*
> *CLAREMONT MCKENNA COLLEGE*

WEAR LAYERS, AND ESPECIALLY a jacket or sweat-shirt that zips in front. Pulling a sweater or sweatshirt over your head involves a lot of movement that is distracting for the people around you. But if you having a zipping jacket, you can take it off without major movements to disrupt the people around you trying to focus!

—LAURA BOUTWELL
WINCHESTER, VIRGINIA
SAT/ACT SCORES: 1410
COLLEGE OF WILLIAM AND MARY

"Do whatever you need to do before the test to calm your nerves. Eat a good breakfast, talk to friends, avoid looking at any prep materials. The hard work is now behind you."

—S.N.
RALEIGH, NORTH CAROLINA
SAT/ACT SCORES: 2390

THE FIRST TIME I TOOK THE TEST I had four strikes against me: I didn't study, my alarm clock didn't go off, I forgot my calculator, and I rushed out of the house without eating breakfast. The next time, I practiced, got my stuff together, enlisted my mom's help in making sure I was up and ate a good breakfast. What a difference—my score went up a hundred points!

—TAMMI COOKS
ST. LOUIS, MISSOURI
WASHINGTON UNIVERSITY IN ST. LOUIS

Wearing earplugs on test day is a great way to eliminate distractions! You won't get fouled up by the ticking clock or by someone else's sniffling.

—*ERICA*
SOUTH ORANGE,
NEW JERSEY
WASHINGTON
UNIVERSITY IN ST.
LOUIS

TO HELP EASE THE STRESS, try to remember that this test is not the only thing that will determine where you go to college. Everyone always puts so much pressure on that one test, and a lot of people lose their cool. The valedictorian of my high school did not score very well, and yet she still got into a great school because of her GPA.

—*S.M.*
MAHWAH, NEW JERSEY
SAT/ACT SCORES: 1310
PENNSYLVANIA STATE UNIVERSITY

· · · · · · · · ·

HAVE SOMEONE DRIVE you to the test and pick you up. Chances are, the testing school is in a somewhat unfamiliar area, and the added stress will not put you in a positive, effective test-taking frame of mind. And after you finish the test, the last thing you feel mentally and physically up to doing is driving home.

—*CAITLIN MYERS*
CINCINNATI, OHIO
SAT/ACT SCORES: 1929/29
MIAMI UNIVERSITY

· · · · · · · · ·

BE SURE TO STAY UPDATED on where your test center is. After I registered they sent me a notice with the location of my testing center. A few weeks later, when I got another notice, I just assumed it was a confirmation of that previous one and didn't look at it closely. Turns out they had moved my test to a different high school, which I didn't find out until the day of the test, when I arrived at the first school and no one was there. I eventually made it to the new location, but it was a really stressful way to start out the day!

—*LAURA*
CINCINNATI, OHIO
SAT/ACT SCORES: 31
FRANCISCAN UNIVERSITY OF STEUBENVILLE

TOP PRE-TEST MISTAKES

Just because you're ready for the SAT doesn't mean you're ready to *take* the SAT. These are some of the most common mistakes made by students on test day:

- Forgetting to bring a calculator, or bringing the wrong calculator

- Forgetting a watch

- Getting distracted

- Forgetting or deciding not to eat

I NEVER REALIZED HOW HUNGRY and thirsty I would get, and I didn't realize that eating wasn't allowed in the testing room. I prepared for this the second time by bringing a granola bar and eating it and getting a drink quickly during the three-minute breaks. I basically learned after taking the SAT for the first time that even the smallest things that occur can make a big difference. Being prepared for the little things that you didn't expect can add up to big point increases.

> —*MATTHEW HABER*
> *HOLLAND, PENNSYLVANIA*
> *SAT/ACT SCORES: 2300*
> *CORNELL UNIVERSITY*

THE SECOND TIME I TOOK IT, I had already decided where I hoped to go to school. So I wore my school-of-choice Washington University shirt for good luck. It worked!

> —*CAITLIN ASTRUE*
> *ST. LOUIS, MISSOURI*
> *WASHINGTON UNIVERSITY IN ST. LOUIS*

RESTED, READY, AND RARING TO GO

Some tips for test day:

EAT, PREFERABLY SOMETHING WITH PROTEIN. If you think you can eat in the morning without giving yourself a stomachache, you'll be glad you did so. Nothing's more distracting than extreme hunger and lightheadedness. If you can add a little protein into your breakfast (eggs, bacon, soy, etc.), it'll help feed your brain.

USE CAFFEINE. Whether it's coffee, tea, or diet soda, caffeine can help keep you alert and perform better. If you don't typically drink anything with caffeine in it, experiment a few weeks in advance rather than risk making yourself anxious, giving yourself a stomachache, or being forced to go to the bathroom constantly.

GET A GOOD NIGHT'S SLEEP FOR SEVERAL NIGHTS BEFORE THE SAT. Try to get to bed at a decent hour on Thursday as well as Friday— being well rested is something that builds up in your system.

STAY RELAXED THE DAY BEFORE THE TEST. Try not to study (very much), party, or do anything illegal the day before you take the SAT. The ideal evening probably consists of a fun, relaxing dinner, some TV or a movie, and then a slightly early bedtime.

DON'T RELY ON WEB SITES like MapQuest for directions to your test-taking site! Call the school itself and speak to a real person there so you can count on getting accurate information. My brother and I got incredibly lost on our way to the test because we got bad directions from an online source. Luckily, we had left early enough that we still got there in time, but it just added more stress to an already stressful day.

> —*TEKLA TOMAN*
> *YOUNGSTOWN, OHIO*
> *SAT/ACT SCORES: 29*
> *XAVIER UNIVERSITY*

. . . .

I'M FROM A SMALL TOWN in Illinois and had to travel two and a half hours to take the test. My parents dropped me off with the approximately 100 other students who were waiting outside the school—but the doors never opened. Later, I found out there were some mixed signals between the SAT people and the school. I rescheduled it for the next month, and I made sure to call the school ahead of time to confirm they were ready.

> —*JASON METCALF*
> *ST. LOUIS, MISSOURI*
> *WASHINGTON UNIVERSITY IN ST. LOUIS*

. . . .

DON'T CRAM THE NIGHT BEFORE; it's just going to ruin your chances for a good night's sleep. The best bet is to study all you can up to the Thursday before the exam, and then just relax on Friday; go have some fun with your friends, then get to bed early. Wake up, eat a good breakfast, and relax. It's a long test, so you will need your energy.

> —*S.M.*
> *MAHWAH, NEW JERSEY*
> *SAT/ACT SCORES: 1310*
> *PENNSYLVANIA STATE UNIVERSITY*

I read a magazine or a newspaper before I took each test to get my mind going and get myself focused.

> —*LAURA ELAINE*
> *GOLDSTICKER*
> *ST. LOUIS,*
> *MISSOURI*
> *SAT/ACT*
> *SCORES: 1800/33*

HAVE BREAKFAST BEFORE YOU GO. I had oatmeal, so I would say have a warm breakfast. And wear a sweater with a T-shirt underneath. Be comfortable; if you are uncomfortable you can't concentrate on the test.

> —*ELISA VIERA*
> *WHITTIER, CALIFORNIA*

• • • • • • • •

Make sure you have nothing else on your mind; the test will require all of your mental attention to finish each section in time.

—*JONATHAN MICHAEL KELLEY CINCINNATI, OHIO SAT/ACT SCORES: 1940 ⚑ UNDECIDED*

I THOUGHT I WAS SO PREPARED for the ACT. I had four No. 2 pencils and six erasers in my purse. I had on comfortable shoes, and I only drank half a cup of water so I wouldn't have to go to the bathroom before or during the exam. But right when it was time for the exam, I got my pencils out of my purse to find them all broken, and my erasers were blue because an ink pen busted in my purse. So I had to interrupt the instructions by sharpening four pencils with a very loud electric pencil sharpener. I heard the proctor breathe deep and say, "It's always one student." I interpreted that to mean it's always somebody who is not prepared. I wanted so badly to prove to her how prepared I was, but my score proved it enough.

> —*CARLA*
> *CHICAGO, ILLINOIS*
> *SAT/ACT SCORES: 27*
> *⚑ UNIVERSITY OF GEORGIA*

• • • • • • • •

CALL AHEAD TO MAKE SURE they are going to start the test on time. At one test session, everyone showed up and the proctor said the test wasn't going to start for a whole hour. Everybody just waited for an entire hour in a big room, getting more and more stressed. It was pretty ridiculous.

> —*RONALD JORDAN HINSON*
> *LENOIR, NORTH CAROLINA*
> *SAT/ACT SCORES: 1940*
> *⚑ CLEMSON UNIVERSITY*

MY SAT-DAY ROUTINE was very specific: I got up early and ran around the block twice, to get my blood pumping. I had my favorite breakfast (eggs and toast), wore my favorite college sweatshirt and used pencils that were my favorite colors (blue and purple). It was all very comforting.

> —*MICHAEL GOODWIN*
> *PROVIDENCE, RHODE ISLAND*
> *SAT/ACT SCORES: 2030*
> *WASHINGTON UNIVERSITY IN ST. LOUIS*

"I always stretched and did some very light exercise before a major test. It helps me to relax, and it spends a little physical energy. The last thing you want is to be antsy at the desk."

> —*PETER WILLIAM FINNOCCHIARO*
> *BALDWINSVILLE, NEW YORK*
> *SAT/ACT SCORES: 2300/32*
> *UNDECIDED*

ON THE DAY OF THE TEST, I made sure to wake up extra early so that I wouldn't be groggy. I ate a good breakfast (salmon and eggs; my mom always made that before a test or a track meet). Also, music helps me wake up and get excited, so I played loud music all the way to the test. Silence would have made me nervous and sluggish.

> —*BLAYNE ALEXANDER*
> *EDMOND, OKLAHOMA*
> *DUKE UNIVERSITY*

ON THE SATURDAY MORNING I was scheduled to take the test, I just happened to check my e-mail. It was a good thing I did because they had changed the location and e-mailed me the new information.

—*MICHELLE WADDELL*
HOLLYWOOD, FLORIDA
WASHINGTON UNIVERSITY IN ST. LOUIS

• • • • • • • • •

BE SURE YOU USE A CALCULATOR MODEL that's approved for use for the SAT. During one test, the proctor took my calculator because it wasn't on their "acceptable" list. I had to finish the rest of the Math section on my own.

—*JOHN STEPHEN REBER*
CINCINNATI, OHIO
SAT/ACT SCORES: 2200
GEORGETOWN UNIVERSITY

Start Your Engines: Taking the Test

*T*he SAT is a long *test, and can seem even longer with slow-speaking proctors, broken wall clocks, unwashed fellow test takers, tiny chair-desks, and children playing loudly just outside the window. In many students' experiences, the test itself would actually be funny if it wasn't so serious. So while you're officially being tested on math, reading, and writing, you're also being tested on your ability to sit in one seat for five hours and perform well despite all of the distractions, annoyances, and inconveniences.*

Just try to remember that students everywhere are dealing with the same things you are, including the nearly unbearable length of the test and all of the petty problems that happen in the testing center. If you're ready for everything that could go wrong and are determined to make the best of it, you may actually end up better off *than those who succumb to test-day distractions.*

Think of it as an opportunity. If you can make it through the SAT successfully, you'll be done. No more bubbles, no more practice tests, no more study sessions. And college—with all of the freedom and excitement that it entails—will be right around the corner. Could there be any greater incentive to make this the most successful morning of your life?

Read on to discover how others successfully navigated test day.

MY PROCTOR WAS ALSO my school advisor. On the day of the SAT, as we entered the testing area, he stood at the top of the stairs and said, loudly, "Julia Kobus, lead everyone to the room." It made me laugh.

> —JULIA KOBUS
> ST. LOUIS, MISSOURI
> SAT/ACT SCORES: 1260/28
> WASHINGTON UNIVERSITY IN ST. LOUIS

• • • • • • • • •

I TOOK THE SAT TWICE, and both times I made it to my room just in time. The first time I took the SAT I looked up my room assignment and I ended up in the wrong room. The second time, I took it at a school and there were other activities going on. When I arrived, there were a bunch of students waiting in the cafeteria. I just assumed that they were all waiting for the rooms to open, but they were just students doing something else. After waiting with them for a while, I had to run upstairs to find my room but fortunately the test hadn't started yet.

> —LOUIS S. WU
> SILVER SPRING, MARYLAND
> SAT/ACT SCORES: 2300
> UNIVERSITY OF MARYLAND

• • • • • • • • •

IF I SKIPPED AN ANSWER I always circled it and made sure to skip it on the bubble sheet. One guy I know skipped the first one and forgot to skip that bubble and therefore put the wrong answer in every bubble for the entire test! He went through all that pain and effort for nothing!

> —ANONYMOUS
> TIBURON, CALIFORNIA
> SAT/ACT SCORES: 1980
> UNIVERSITY OF CALIFORNIA, LOS ANGELES

Don't look up. Once you start looking up you might notice someone else is sweating it and that can make you nervous.

> —DAVID
> ST. LOUIS, MISSOURI
> SAT/ACT SCORES: 2020/29
> UNIVERSITY OF WISCONSIN

HEAD**LINES**
Best Advice and Top Tips

- Expect the unexpected; students have been known to get physically ill at these tests!
- Don't let clueless proctors and cheating students distract you; stay focused on your work.
- If you finish a section early and you have a few extra minutes, close your eyes and prepare yourself for the sections ahead.

LIKE MOST THINGS IN LIFE, the most difficult part of the SAT is preparation. Believe it or not, it is probably the shortest three hours of your life. While you may have spent years studying and practicing for the SATs, the actual exam should go quickly. The quiet energy of the room will help keep you focused while you try to ignore your quick-beating heart and perform at your highest potential. The key is, stay calm, stay alert, and do your best.

—*BETH LORI WECKSELL*
GREAT NECK, NEW YORK
SAT/ACT SCORES: 1370
TUFTS UNIVERSITY

• • • • • • • •

WHENEVER I KNEW I HAD only five minutes left, and I hadn't finished reading a section, rather than finish it, I went straight to the definition questions that I knew I could answer even without reading the entire portion.

—*WILLIAM ECKLEY*
ST. LOUIS, MISSOURI
SAT/ACT SCORES: 1910/19
HAMILTON COLLEGE

THE NIGHT BEFORE I TOOK THE ACT, I took practice tests all night long. I was exhausted the
next morning. During the test, I finished a few
parts really early, so I decided to take a nap. I
fell half-asleep, and had a dream that I was
walking on ice. I slipped on the ice in the dream
and jolted upright awake in my seat. It was
embarrassing to find that everyone in the test
room was staring at me.

> —*GREGORY JAMES FRIEND*
> *EVANSTON, ILLINOIS*
> *SAT/ACT SCORES: 2160/32*
> *NORTHWESTERN UNIVERSITY*

"Sometimes you make friends
during these tests. It's such a
stressful situation that it brings
people together. You just start
talking and later you Facebook
each other and become friends.
My older brother actually dated
a girl that he met at the SAT."

> —*ANONYMOUS*
> *CLAYTON, MISSOURI*
> *SAT/ACT SCORES: 2060/32*

TAKE DEEP BREATHS and take comfort in what you
already know.

> —*JENNIFER STEWART*
> *MURFREESBORO, TENNESSEE*
> *SAT/ACT SCORES: 25*
> *MIDDLE TENNESSEE STATE UNIVERSITY*

Sometimes the proctor will tell you when you have five minutes left, but not always. I brought a clock just in case.

—ANONYMOUS
  ST. LOUIS,
  MISSOURI
  SAT/ACT SCORES:
  2290/35
  🏛 UNDECIDED

DURING MY SAT, the proctor instructed us to save all questions until the end of the directions. She reads out all the instructions, and at the end a boy raises his hand and says, "I'm supposed to be taking the SAT II. What should I do?" We were all laughing our heads off because he had clearly known for 10 minutes that he was in the wrong room and didn't say anything because he didn't want to interrupt. There are obviously exceptions to every rule, and I think most people don't really anticipate how much being nervous can interfere with things like common sense!

—BECKY
  NEWTON, MASSACHUSETTS
  SAT/ACT SCORES: 2290
  🏛 SWARTHMORE COLLEGE

· · · · · · · ·

I WAS IN LINE TO TAKE THE SAT, and the guy standing directly behind me ran out of the line and threw up! I was just glad it wasn't on me. It actually sharpened my focus to realize how much he was worried. I thought, "Oh, wow, I really do need to do well."

—LAURA ELAINE GOLDSTICKER
  ST. LOUIS, MISSOURI
  SAT/ACT SCORES: 1800/33

· · · · · · · ·

BEFORE THE TEST, everyone was waiting in line to go into the testing room. I was behind this guy who forgot his calculator and his driver's license—turns out he left them in his friend's car. Well, the lady letting the kids in would not permit him entry, and he made a huge scene. He then whipped out his cell phone and screamed at his friend to come bring him his stuff. (He screamed other things too, but I won't discuss them here.)

—RYAN BATES
  HUDSON, WISCONSIN

SAT HORROR STORIES #111 & #112

DURING THE VERBAL SECTION OF THE TEST, I finished one of the reading comprehension sets that ended at the top of the page. There was such a big blank space after that particular excerpt and set of questions that I assumed that was the end of the section and put my pencil down. I was used to finishing with time to spare, at least on the Verbal section. When the proctor told us it was time to move to the next section, I turned the page, only to find another set of reading comprehension questions! Having skipped a significant number of questions, I had to retake the test a couple months later. I was so frustrated because I had wasted all that time, and money! My dad was mad at me too. It was pretty traumatizing.

—*MEGAN NOWAK*
COLUMBUS, OHIO
SAT/ACT SCORES: 1380
MIAMI UNIVERSITY

• • • • • • • • •

ONE TIME I GOT REALLY ANXIOUS BEFORE A TEST and I took this pill call Klonopin. It's a prescription pill that you take to calm down. I couldn't stop shaking and throwing up before my test, so I just took it. Well, I got about 20 minutes into the test when I realized the test pages were turning colors. I just sat there and watched the pages change colors for a while. I stayed for the whole test and I don't even remember if I finished it because I was too interested in watching the pages change colors. Never resort to a one-time fix to calm you down. I'm on anti-anxiety pills that are daily and those are fine. But I wouldn't take any medication beforehand that you don't have a lot of experience with.

—*RAYNA*
NEEDHAM, MASSACHUSETTS
SAT/ACT SCORES: 2280
CLAREMONT MCKENNA COLLEGE

NOTHING SHOULD BE A SURPRISE when you are taking the actual SAT if you have practiced and prepared for it. The test should look almost identical to all the practice tests you have been doing.

—*ANONYMOUS*
NEW YORK, NEW YORK
NEW YORK UNIVERSITY

I AM FROM ILLINOIS, and the state-mandated ACT came up in April, and since I had by then gotten a very good SAT score, I didn't really care about the results. My friend and I were sitting in the back of the room, goofing off before the test. The teacher came over and scolded us and said, "You guys need to concentrate." He was pretty mad. Turns out we got the two highest scores in the school. I got a 35, which is even better than my SAT score. I think that's a big thing that students need to overcome: it doesn't pay to be nervous. I always told myself that those tests weren't really that high pressured, because you can take them multiple times.

—*ANONYMOUS*
ILLINOIS
SAT/ACT SCORES: 2240/35
YALE UNIVERSITY

THE NEW SAT WAS JUST SO LONG. I remember sitting there and just not being able to look at the pages anymore. I even ended up accidentally skipping one of the sections. We went on a break, and when we came back they told us to turn to section six and I was still on section five. I was like, "Oh crap!" It just left me emotionally and intellectually drained.

—*ALICE HU*
REDMOND, WASHINGTON
SAT/ACT SCORES: 2260
STANFORD UNIVERSITY

THE SCHOOL I TOOK THE SAT in decided to have their basketball playoffs on the same day for their middle school. It was awful! Through most of the test I heard the ball dribbling on the pavement right next to the window. After the test I called the complaint line for testing conditions on SAT days and reported it. Hopefully that will prevent it from happening again because it was really unfair.

> —*JOHN*
> *VENICE, CALIFORNIA*
> *SAT/ACT SCORES: 2290*
> *UNDECIDED*

THE SECOND TIME I took the SAT I had just gotten back from Washington D.C. and I forgot that I had to take the SAT until the night before. I remember thinking, "Oh my God, I have an SAT tomorrow!" I actually did well on it and I think it's because I didn't have any time to think about it and create anxiety around it. It's just about being in the right mind frame so you can focus your knowledge into answering the questions instead of having your brain shut down from anxiety that can block the information.

> —*LIVIA ROMANO*
> *SAN DIEGO, CALIFORNIA*
> *SAT/ACT SCORES: 2020*
> *CLAREMONT MCKENNA COLLEGE*

DON'T SKIP AHEAD! When I took the SAT in October, a guy in my room went ahead to the next section since he finished early. The proctor caught him, kicked him out, and informed us that the College Board would actually put in his score report to colleges that he cheated on the test.

> —*ANONYMOUS*
> *SIMI VALLEY, CALIFORNIA*
> *SAT/ACT SCORES: 2230*
> *UNDECIDED*

Don't see it as an opportunity to learn. You have to have the SAT mindset: you just read the questions and do what the test asks.

—*WILLIAM ECKLEY*
ST. LOUIS,
MISSOURI
SAT/ACT
SCORES: 1910/19
HAMILTON
COLLEGE

JUGGLING DEMANDS

Last October, I had to wear my cross-country uniform and warmups during the exam because I had a meet right after. I arranged to take my test at the high school where the meet was held so I could be there as soon as possible. However, many of my teammates had to drive a good distance to get to the meet after the test and cut it pretty close.

The nearly five-hour-long test proved to be a difficult pre-race activity for us all. Not only do you get extremely stiff and tired during the exam, but your eating and sleeping habits are all thrown off; instead of being able to wake up four hours before race time and have a light breakfast, I had to get up eight hours before the race and couldn't really eat anything at my normal time because it was during testing. Also, the night prior to the test and meet was a huge annual football game that I had to attend because I play for the pep band. So basically the night before taking an important exam and running in a big meet, I was stuck out in the cold until 10:30 p.m.—not the ideal situation!

—Chris DelGrosso
Moorestown, New Jersey
SAT/ACT Scores: 2050
Emerson College

I HAD ONE BOY IN MY TEST that got so nervous, before the test, he ran to the trashcan and threw up. After getting the test, he laid his head down on the desk and we later found out he passed out due to nervousness and stress!

—*CASEY PONTIOUS*
LOCUST GROVE, OKLAHOMA
FREE WILL BAPTIST BIBLE COLLEGE

• • • • • • • •

THE PROCTORS WERE REALLY BITCHY during my exam, and kept making annoying noises. One of them kept walking around, bumping into boxes, and his shoes had clicky sounds. I gave them really cold stares when resting my eyes from reading questions, and I was able to release some of my frustration. When I was taking practice tests, I shut myself in a room so there really weren't many noises, so it was really different when taking the test with 30 other people.

—*YUEYUE GUO*
CUMBERLAND, RHODE ISLAND
SAT/ACT SCORES: 2220
UNDECIDED

• • • • • • • •

THE WORST PART ABOUT TAKING the SAT is the length. Just sitting through the whole thing was a challenge in itself. After a while I just couldn't concentrate. I was on the last Reading section and I got to the point where I would read the entire section and not even remember what I read. I panicked a little bit, then forced myself to concentrate and went back over it.

—*ELIZABETH*
DENVER, COLORADO
SAT/ACT SCORES: 2100
CLAREMONT MCKENNA COLLEGE

I think some people worry about the test too much and hype it up to be this big monster. But the reality is that it is just a test.

—*ANDREW MICHAEL RIZZI*
BALDWIN, NEW YORK
SAT/ACT SCORES: 1390
SYRACUSE UNIVERSITY

Consider

I FELT BAD FOR THE PERSON sitting next to me during my exam. About a half hour into the test he put his head down on his desk and fell asleep and didn't complete the test. He didn't even try.

—*EMMA*
WASHINGTON, D.C.
SAT/ACT SCORES: 1890
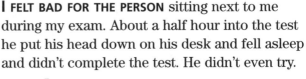 *PITZER COLLEGE*

Be prepared to sit and think for a good three hours!

—*EMILY*
NEW YORK, NEW YORK
CARNEGIE MELLON UNIVERSITY

I TOOK THE SAT in two very different environments: a prestigious private school, and an urban public school in the city. It seemed to me that the kids in the first setting were taking it more seriously, and somehow it was easier for me to concentrate in that setting. Even though it was my second time and I theoretically was more prepared, I scored lower in the city classroom. I don't want to sound snobby, but try to take the test in the best setting possible, where the kids are the most serious about it.

—*ANONYMOUS*
TIBURON, CALIFORNIA
SAT/ACT SCORES: 1980
UNIVERSITY OF CALIFORNIA, LOS ANGELES

THE FIRST TIME I TOOK THE SAT, I took it at a different location from my high school. I was already terrified, but having to go to a different school was frightening. I was nervous and uncomfortable the entire time. The second time I took it at my high school and I did much better. I don't know if it was because of the comfort of being at my own school.

—*JOCELYN*
BEVERLY HILLS, CALIFORNIA
SAT/ACT SCORES: 1540
UNIVERSITY OF ARIZONA

SUMMARY: NOT A FUN EXPERIENCE

Sitting for four hours was horrible. I was very miserable by the end of the test. I wanted to leave and I wanted to stop taking the test. I was hungry, my butt was hurting, my arms were hurting, and I was tired. The information is not extremely difficult. You are placed in this high-pressure environment where everything is timed; you do one section in this amount of time, then another section, then you take a short break, come back and do another section. If they would make it more of a relaxing atmosphere it would be much better. Half of the time the proctors don't even know what they are doing, and that is really frustrating because when they aren't doing their jobs right we end up sitting there longer. I remember waiting for them to finish their paperwork for a long time. I remember feeling that they were totally incompetent and should have definitely been trained better in test administration. I was appalled at how long it took them to hand out the test books and fill out the forms. I was in there an hour later than I should have been.

—*LIVIA ROMANO*
SAN DIEGO, CALIFORNIA
SAT/ACT SCORES: 2020
CLAREMONT MCKENNA COLLEGE

EXPECT THE UNEXPECTED

You should be ready for anything to happen on test day. *Anything*.

CLUELESS PROCTORS: While most of the people hired to monitor the SAT do a great job, sometimes they mess up. Try not to be fazed. It will be tough to do anything about minor mistakes, but if the proctor is doing something very wrong (e.g. not giving you enough time for a section, or not allowing you to use a calculator that meets the requirements) you should speak up.

CHEATING STUDENTS: Someone might try to look at your paper or ask you for the answer to a question. Act appropriately, and realize that being caught cheating can have disastrous consequences.

TIME PROBLEMS. In addition to the proctor making a timing mistake, the wall clock may be broken or other test-takers may loudly complain (even incorrectly) about how time is announced.

LOUD DISRUPTIONS BY OTHER STUDENTS. Someone might freak out during the test, start an argument with a proctor, or otherwise disrupt the rest of the room. The proctor might not know how to appropriately deal with the situation. Stay focused.

I THOUGHT THAT DRINKING VITAMIN water was a good idea but then I really had to go to the bathroom and couldn't leave! I was ready to burst at the seams and I think that may have been distracting for me. Don't drink a lot before the test and be careful—those little sips can add up and you'll be sitting with your legs crossed!

—*STEFANIE LAMPRECHT*
TIBURON, CALIFORNIA
SAT/ACT SCORES: 1800
SANTA CLARA UNIVERSITY

. . . .

66 Don't be afraid to request something. During the SAT, there was a clock hanging in the back of the classroom. I asked the proctor to move the clock to the front, and she ended up hanging it on a tack on a bulletin board. 99

—*LAUREN*
POTOMAC, MARYLAND
SAT/ACT SCORES: 33
CORNELL UNIVERSITY

. . . .

IT WAS CRAZY. During the test, some kid threw up on the floor, and my worst fear in the world is puking, so I about died when that happened. Be ready for anything!

—*ALEXXA CONDON*
CHANNAHON, ILLINOIS
SOUTHERN ILLINOIS UNIVERSITY, CARBONDALE

I HAD A KID SITTING NEXT to me who was very verbal. Every time he typed something into the system he would say it out loud. You might think, 'That's a good way to get answers.', but the people around you are not all doing the same sections. So while I was trying to read he was mumbling something about math.

—JESSICA
DALLAS, TEXAS
RICE UNIVERSITY

• • • • • • • • •

THE DAY I TOOK THE SAT, I was sick as a dog. My nose wouldn't stop running and I was hopped up on Dayquil. I wasn't too worried about that distracting me from doing well on the test. In my experience, the less seriously I take the exam questions, the better I do. But, I did end up using up both Kleenex boxes in the exam room all by myself.

—BRYAN EDWARD TAYLOR
EVANSTON, ILLINOIS
SAT/ACT SCORES: 2200/35
NORTHWESTERN UNIVERSITY

• • • • • • • • •

DURING THE EXAM, I looked around and saw kids who looked serious. I felt like we were all competing for one prize, and I became intimidated. So I closed my eyes and did a quick prayer. Afterwards, I mumbled to myself, saying, "This is it. There is no going back now. Expect the worst and hope for the best. There is nothing you can't do. You are just as smart as anyone in this room. You worked hard. You will get a good score; no, not a good score, but a great score." That encouraged me until my fifth reading passage, where I got bored out of my mind.

—MARQUITA REESE
CHICAGO, ILLINOIS
SAT/ACT SCORES: 23
CHICAGO STATE UNIVERSITY

WHEN YOU FINISH A SECTION EARLY ...

Frankly, you shouldn't be finishing *any* section of the SAT with lots of extra time to spare. It's a hard test. But if you *do* finish early, even with just a few extra minutes, here's what you can do:

CHECK TOUGH PROBLEMS FIRST. It's nearly impossible to go back and catch silly mistakes with just a few minutes to spare. Instead, you should mark the most difficult questions as you proceed and go back to them at the end if you have extra time.

ON THE ESSAY, CHECK FOR ERRORS. Make sure you used punctuation properly, didn't make any of the grammar mistakes that sometimes trouble you, and write legibly throughout the essay.

DON'T BE AFRAID TO TAKE A SHORT BREAK. If you have just a few minutes and don't see a good way to use your time, go ahead and take 1-2 minutes to close your eyes, focus, and prepare for what you know lies ahead.

IF YOU HAVE A COLD on the morning of the test, be sure to take a decongestant before you go in. I had a horrible cold during one of my test sessions, and I wasn't allowed to bring tissues in with me. I spent the whole time sniffling and sneezing—it not only distracted me, it also distracted all the people around me, but there was nothing I could do about it!

—*LAURA*
CINCINNATI, OHIO
SAT/ACT SCORES: 31
FRANCISCAN UNIVERSITY OF STEUBENVILLE

• • • • • • • •

FOR ME, CONCENTRATING on the SAT in a room full of people was something I had effectively been doing my entire life—in sports. It was just like shooting free throws in a full gymnasium or concentrating on a curveball despite all eyes on the field being on you. I was very nervous the day before the SAT and just as apprehensive the day of, but once the teacher says "Go," there simply is no time for nerves.

—*DREW SILVERMAN*
ELKINS PARK, PENNSYLVANIA
SAT/ACT SCORES: 1410
SYRACUSE UNIVERSITY

• • • • • • • •

I WAS TAKING THE TEST and we had our first break. For some whacky reason I had brought a huge Asian pear to eat. I ate it and we went back to testing. I was doing math and suddenly my stomach started grumbling very loudly so that other kids could hear it. It was a little embarrassing once I noticed other kids snickering. I'm going to take the test again, and next time I'll eat a better breakfast and bring a granola or something.

—*AMAR PANJWANI*
APPLE VALLEY, CALIFORNIA
UNDECIDED

I'M A JEANS-AND-SANDALS TYPE of girl so I went to my SAT dressed comfortably. But don't dress too sloppy, or you'll get too relaxed and probably fall asleep, like one guy next to me, who came to the test in his pajamas. And don't get too dress up because you might get uptight. And please, no heels. I remember one girl who kept going to the bathroom, and I can still hear her three-inch heels clicking in my ear. I'm sure I got a couple of answers wrong listening to those heels.

—*BETH HARVEY*
CHICAGO, ILLINOIS
KENTUCKY WESLEYAN COLLEGE

"Bringing a healthy snack for the longer breaks really helps you to refocus when your energy level gets low after sitting at a desk for hours."

—*TERRAHNEY WILSON*
LITHONIA, GEORGIA
SAT/ACT SCORES: 1950
UNDECIDED

TO ME, TAKING THE SAT itself was like a scene out of a horror story. Just taking that really long test and having the feeling that this is going to be a huge factor in the acceptance process gave me nightmares. Anything that students can do to de-stress during that time, whether it be working out, taking a walk, or doing yoga, is a good idea.

—*ANONYMOUS*
BURBANK, CALIFORNIA
SAT/ACT SCORES: 870/19
PEPPERDINE UNIVERSITY

WHEN I TOOK THE SAT, I made sure to not be distracted by the others around me. I made sure to stay calm and confident in the answers I thought were correct, and I made sure to block out all distractions. I accomplished this by maintaining self-control, keeping my head pointed straight down, and thinking of the task at hand, which was answering the questions. I think I may have ADD because I sometimes have trouble concentrating, but I have to tell myself that there's nothing else around me but me, the test, and the chair I'm sitting on.

—*TIM*
PHOENIX, ARIZONA
SAT/ACT SCORES: 2130
UNDECIDED

• • • • • • • • •

RIGHT BEFORE WE WERE about to start the first section (the essay), a girl came in late after running about a mile from her car. The teacher allowed her to sign in quickly but she was breathing very hard for about another five minutes. I had to write my first two paragraphs with the background noise of someone who sounded like they were suffering from asphyxiation! I thought it actually lightened the mood a bit, since everyone else seemed so intense.

—*STEPHANIE*
NEW FAIRFIELD, CONNECTICUT
SAT/ACT SCORES: 2300
UNDECIDED

Anticipation: Getting Your Scores

A couple of weeks after you take the SAT, you'll open your mailbox (or your e-mail inbox) and your scores will be waiting for you. If the score is higher than what you expected, or what you figure you need to get into the college of your choice, you'll be elated. So will your parents, who themselves feel every bit as invested in this process as you do. There will be celebratory dinners, congratulatory phone calls, and a feeling of accomplishment and relief that's difficult to describe.

If the score is lower than you had hoped, you'll need to reassess your situation. Could you have done better? Would you likely do better if *you took the test again? Is it time to acknowledge that you may need to apply to a different set of colleges?*

Don't forget that whether you scored above or below expectations— or did exactly as well as you thought you would—your friends are all going through a similar ordeal. Their scores will be higher or lower than yours, and their expectations will be met, exceeded, or drastically disappointed. For many students, this is the most emotionally draining part of the high school experience. Try your best to remember how they may be feeling and reduce any tension or awkwardness.

Here's how others handled the anticipation, and the moments they received the numbers that would help decide the next step in their lives.

EVEN THOUGH OTHER STUDENTS might act nonchalant about their scores, they care a lot more than they let on. I was on a mission trip in Peru once when the scores were posted, and there was only one computer to look them up. There were 10 of us standing in line to get on there and check our scores, and we were all nervous—even the guys who said they didn't care.

—*JOHN STEPHEN REBER*
CINCINNATI, OHIO
SAT/ACT SCORES: 2200
GEORGETOWN UNIVERSITY

Even though my school didn't put too much emphasis on the SAT, I was still a basket case while I was waiting for my SAT scores.

—*R.H.*
LONG BEACH, CALIFORNIA
SAT/ACT SCORES: 1200
CALIFORNIA STATE UNIVERSITY, LONG BEACH

I GOT A 2360 ON THE SAT the first time I took it, and as much as I would like a 2400, I'm not going to go through that again. I decided that it wasn't worth it. With my score I knew I would be in the top 25 percent of applicants to my schools of choice. Look at the colleges you want to go to and if your scores are significantly lower than the top 25 percent of applicants, I would advise doing more prep for the SAT and retaking it. Otherwise, you don't need a perfect score; stop worrying and go celebrate.

—*PATTY LU*
TINTON FALLS, NEW JERSEY
SAT/ACT SCORES: 2360
UNDECIDED

IF YOU GET A 2300 OR BETTER on your SAT, don't retake it. When you look at your report, you get your actual score and then you get a range of how you would score if you took the test multiple times. I got a 780 on the Math and my range was something like 750 to 800. To me this means that colleges understand and realize that scores in a certain range mean the same thing.

—*BRIAN WU*
CORONA, CALIFORNIA
SAT/ACT SCORES: 2360
UNDECIDED

HEADLINES
Best Advice and Top Tips

- Remember: It's not whether or not you received the score you wanted; it's whether or not your score will get you into a good school.
- While waiting, plan what steps you'll take if the score is lower than you want it to be.

THE ACT SCORES CAME in an envelope, so you got that extra rush. When I saw the score I barely believed it, since I hadn't really studied for the ACT and wasn't taking it that seriously on test day. There wasn't much of a celebration because I don't think that my parents or my friends really understood the significance of it. I mean, there is maybe one person in a thousand who can get a 35 on the ACT, but to everyone else it was more like "Oh, cool." And, the fact that they scored lower didn't exactly put them in a celebratory mood. I mean, I think everyone was happy for me, but in this town, for better or worse, we celebrate beating the next town over in football, not test scores on any level.

—*ANONYMOUS*
ILLINOIS
SAT/ACT SCORES: 2240/35
YALE UNIVERSITY

I WOKE UP AT 5 A.M. to look at my scores. I was very happy with the results and my parents were thrilled. Getting a good score made me more excited about college. But then my friend called and he got a 2280. That was a bit disheartening, since he is looking at the same schools I am, but in the end I was still very happy with my score. I am not a bitter person and I was extremely excited for him. Someone will always do better than you, so there is no need to be arrogant and self centered. Just be happy for your friends if they score better than you do.

—*TIM*
PHOENIX, ARIZONA
SAT/ACT SCORES: 2130
UNDECIDED

"The best way to prepare for getting your test scores back is to set reasonable goals for yourself in the first place. Setting goals too high often leads to discouraging moments."

—*CHRISTINE TODD*
VERO BEACH, FLORIDA
SAT/ACT SCORES: 2250
NORTHWESTERN UNIVERSITY

I WAS PERFECTLY HAPPY. I wanted an 800 on Verbal, but 770 was enough to get me where I wanted to go.

—*ANONYMOUS*
BROOKLYN, NEW YORK

Remember: This is the last time in your life that any-one will care what you scored on the SAT.

—*N.*
NEW YORK,
NEW YORK

THE MOMENT I SAW THE 800 on Math, I realized it was worth it. If it's your first time taking the SAT, like this was for me, don't worry about it at all. It's good that you took it once, even if you didn't get the score you wanted, because now you know what the test is like and some of the tricks the College Board throws at you. And yes, we did celebrate the 800. We went out to dinner that day. My dad isn't an awfully emotional person, but he seemed extremely pleased with that score.

—*NEIL SHAH*
ENCINO, CALIFORNIA
SAT/ACT SCORES: 2230
UNDECIDED

• • • • • • • •

I TOOK THE SAT TWO TIMES. My Verbal score went down the second time (due to an error in skipping a whole section by mistake!) but my Math went up and was the reason I retook the exam. The great thing about the SAT is that schools combine your best score on all tests. For me, this worked out wonderfully. I suggest that students take the SAT two to three times, unless they do exceptionally well the first time, or have no intention of studying before the next exam. A score is "good enough" if it reaches the median SAT score of students admitted to the school you would like to attend.

—*BETH LORI WECKSELL*
GREAT NECK, NEW YORK
SAT/ACT SCORES: 1370
TUFTS UNIVERSITY

KNOW WHEN TO BE HAPPY

My standards for myself are a bit high, but I really wanted to get at least a 2100 on the SAT. That seemed to be the magic number that everyone wanted to beat, or at least everyone in my circle of friends. On my first try I ended up with a 2010, or a 670 in every subject. I was a bit confused at first, because I really thought that I had done better, but I had underestimated how much of the curved scoring determines the score. For example, only now I know that on some tests, missing as few as three math questions can knock you down somewhere into the low 700s, where as when I took the test the first time, my mentality was, "Oh, it's okay if I skip these three; it can't hurt my score that badly!" The ones that I skipped were usually the ones I didn't have time to get to at the end of the sections. I'm not sure how I over-came the disappointment; actually I think I just settled with it. The next time I took the test and got my scores, I was definitely surprised, especially by my Critical Reading score, which was a 780. I was so sure that would be my worst section, but Math was the worst, because I only improved by 20 points, to a 690. Writing went up, too. My parents wished that I could have done better, but I beat my personal goal, so I was happy.

—MICHAEL
SAN DIEGO, CALIFORNIA
SAT/ACT SCORES: 2190
🏠 UNDECIDED

I celebrated on the inside.

—*MICHAEL*
SAN DIEGO,
CALIFORNIA
SAT/ACT
SCORES: 2190
 *UNDECIDED*

WELL, I DIDN'T REALLY CELEBRATE when I got my scores. I was happy about Verbal and Math, but I didn't want to make it that obvious, because I had no idea how my other friends did, so I just said, I did okay. I was actually aiming for 2200+, so I was annoyed when I just missed that by 10 points. I'd considered starting a bonfire but I thought some people from the other years might appreciate my SAT books more. It turns out that one of my friends had her October SAT scores delayed by more than a month, and nearly had her Cornell early-decision application killed, so in the end I was relieved that I actually got my scores, even without the extra 10 points.

—*QUINCY CHUCK*
HONG KONG
SAT/ACT SCORES: 2190
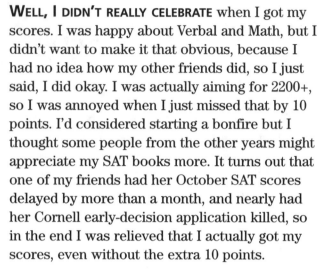 *UNDECIDED*

• • • • • • • • •

I HEARD RUMORS THAT the scores would be posted before 8 a.m., which is the time the College Board says they will be up. I set my alarm to go off every two hours starting at midnight. Every time it went off, I got up and refreshed the page. At 5:15 a.m., when the scores were finally posted, I screamed for my parents, and they were really happy too. I really wasn't expecting to score that high because I wasn't feeling too confident after I took the test, so it was a pleasant surprise. Over the weekend we went out to dinner, but that night my dad brought home a cheesecake and chocolate, my two favorite foods.

—*DEEPTI KALLURI*
ACTON, MASSACHUSETTS
SAT/ACT SCORES: 2240
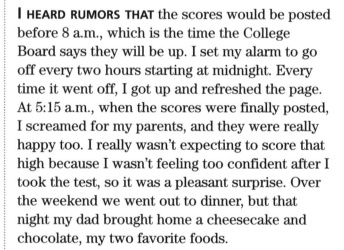 *UNDECIDED*

THOUGH STANDARDIZED TEST scores aren't everything, I was pretty excited when I got my scores, I must confess that I was exponentially more excited when I got into college. I didn't really celebrate; maybe a sigh of relief. I actually think that too much emphasis is placed on things like SATs these days. Doing well on the SAT is obviously important to college admissions, but they are only the product of a few hours of work in a single day. I think that people have to put that into perspective more, and then maybe they would be less stressed out about doing well on the SAT themselves.

—*MATTHEW HABER*
HOLLAND, PENNSYLVANIA
SAT/ACT SCORES: 2300
CORNELL UNIVERSITY

• • • • • • • •

I CELEBRATED AS SOON AS I left the test room. We have a tradition in our family: after a test, no matter how well or poorly we did, we always go out to eat and have fun. Surviving a three-hour test is an accomplishment in itself. Of course, getting the scores was pretty sweet, too. But I was away from my family doing research when I got them, so I was just like "hmm ... 2390. Pretty good. I think I'll go run some more trials now."

—*JESSICA*
BOCA RATON, FLORIDA
SAT/ACT SCORES: 2390
CALIFORNIA INSTITUTE OF TECHNOLOGY

"Not everything that counts can be counted and not everything that can be counted counts."

—*ALBERT EINSTEIN*

ARE YOU DONE YET?

I DECIDED I WAS DONE TAKING SATS after my third try. I have read and been told repeatedly that college admissions officers shun students who have taken the test more than three times. Also, my composite score was now in the median ranges of some of my most competitive prospective colleges. I still would like to increase my score. But I think everyone is interested in having the perfect score. I decided I was done with standardized testing, and am no longer concerned about my score.

> —*KEVIN WANDREI*
> *ADAMS, MASSACHUSETTS*
> *SAT/ACT SCORES: 1260/28*
> *UNIVERSITY OF SOUTHERN CALIFORNIA*

• • • • • • • •

TAKE THE TEST AT LEAST TWICE and then decide if it could help you to take it again. If you take it twice and your scores are roughly the same, chances are they're not going to change much again. But if you take it twice and they're dramatically different, it may be worth it to try one more time.

> —*CHRISTIE*
> *CINCINNATI, OHIO*
> *SAT/ACT SCORES: 2120*
> *UNIVERSITY OF CHARLESTON*

• • • • • • • •

I ALWAYS HAD A PLAN B if I my ACT scores were below 26, which they were. I made sure I was in the top 10 percent of my class. I did community service. I did two summers of college tours around the country. That way, the College Board would know that that I was a smart, verstatile, and ambitious student, not just a good national standardized test taker.

> —*KEVISHA ITSON*
> *CHICAGO, ILLINOIS*
> *SAT/ACT SCORES: 20*
> *UNIVERSITY OF ILLINOIS, URBANA-CHAMPAIGN*

I THINK YOU SHOULD TAKE THE SAT TWO TIMES. I didn't do that well the first time, but I didn't take it hard because I don't think the scores have anything to do with who I am and do not indicate how smart I am. I had really good school grades so I was putting a lot of weight on those. I was upset, but I didn't think it was the end of my life. I checked my scores at school and was like "Oh well, so I'm not a test taker." I told my parents and they were just like me, they have a similar attitude to mine. I wasn't scared that my scores were going to hold me back. I ended up taking it again and did much better. After the second time I stopped because I didn't think that any amount of studying would improve my scores after that. My sister will be taking hers soon and I would definitely tell her to take it twice. I do believe you improve your scores the second time because you are more confident about what to expect. By the third time I think you reach a plateau, and to increase your scores by ten or twenty points just isn't worth all of the stress and time.

> —*JOCELYN*
> *BEVERLY HILLS, CALIFORNIA*
> *SAT/ACT SCORES: 1540*
> *UNIVERSITY OF ARIZONA*

· · · · · · · · ·

I ONLY TOOK THE TEST TWO TIMES. I was actually quite elated with my second score and would not have dreamed of taking it again. My mindset afterward was that if a 2300 wasn't going to get me into a school, then I wasn't meant to go there. If you feel that you have done the best that you possibly can, embrace your scores and be proud of your accomplishments!

> —*STEPHANIE*
> *NEW FAIRFIELD, CONNECTICUT*
> *SAT/ACT SCORES: 2300*
> *UNDECIDED*

I ONLY TOOK THE SATs ONCE. My score the first time was in the range of schools I was applying to and I was happy with my score.

—*C.B.*
NEW YORK, NEW YORK
SAT/ACT SCORES: 1250
SYRACUSE UNIVERSITY

• • • • • • • •

IT'S NOT WORTH IT TO TAKE THE TEST over if you think your scores won't improve too much. I took the test once and I know I could have done better if I had taken it a second time, however I thought that it wasn't worth going through that huge and long process again just for another 50 points or so.

—*JESSICA*
DALLAS, TEXAS
RICE UNIVERSITY

• • • • • • • •

I TOOK THE SAT TWICE BECAUSE my score wasn't good enough to get me into the college I wanted to go to the first time I took it. The second time I took it my scores increased. I didn't study more, I just think having taken it once made me feel more at ease the second time. I think it's a good idea to use your first time as a warmup.

—*TIFFANY*
SHERMAN OAKS, CALIFORNIA
SAT/ACT SCORES: 1910
CLAREMONT MCKENNA COLLEGE

I WAS HOPING TO GET AT LEAST A 30 on the ACT, which would "seal the deal." When I got the 33, I pretty much screamed for 15 minutes straight, calling everyone that I knew. I even ran outside and stood in the middle of my court and yelled "I'm going to college!" That night, my parents and I went to the Cheesecake Factory and I celebrated with a delicious carrot cheesecake.

—*LAUREN*
POTOMAC, MARYLAND
SAT/ACT SCORES: 33
CORNELL UNIVERSITY

• • • • • • • •

IT'S A GOOD IDEA to have at least one SAT and two or three SAT IIs done by the end of your junior year. This way, if you are dissatisfied with your scores, you can get a few retakes in by the beginning of your senior year. Keep in mind that you will not see your October SAT scores before most top colleges' early-decision deadlines. Many schools will accept scores from October and even November, but you will not be able to evaluate your chances if you're using those scores.

—*MICHAEL WYMBS*
BEACH HAVEN, NEW JERSEY
SAT/ACT SCORES: 2260

• • • • • • • •

I COVERED THE SCREEN WITH MY HAND and slowly pulled it down to see the scores one by one and the first thing I saw was a composite 33, so I was quite happy with that. After that, I casually mentioned it to all my friends and secretly glowed inside when they were ecstatic at my great score.

—*JAKE M. KENNEDY*
HICKORY HILLS, ILLINOIS
SAT/ACT SCORES: 2100/33
UNIVERSITY OF SOUTHERN CALIFORNIA

WHEN I GOT A LOW SAT SCORE I really tried to look at the bigger picture. I knew that this would be a huge factor in my college admissions process, but I leveled with myself saying I still have two more times to take it and SAT scores are not the only thing the colleges base their decisions on. The next time I took the SAT, I reviewed some SAT prep material and it raised my score.

—*ANONYMOUS*
BURBANK, CALIFORNIA
SAT/ACT SCORES: 870/19
PEPPERDINE UNIVERSITY

. . . .

THE FIRST TIME I TOOK THE SAT, I did not receive such a good score. I already knew that I was a victim of test anxiety, but I did not give up. I took courses and got textbooks to help enhance my score. I had to realize I wasn't competing with everyone else's scores, I had to compete with myself first. That is how I cheered myself up, and by doing so, I was able to increase my SAT score.

—*BRITTANY ELYSE GRAHAM*
WEST CHESTER, PENNSYLVANIA
SAT/ACT SCORES: 890/21
INDIANA UNIVERSITY OF PENNSYLVANIA

. . . .

THE WAITING PERIOD FOR SCORES was the worst of all. I could barely type or move the mouse when I finally checked online for my scores. A load had been taken off my shoulders, and I went on with the rest of my high school career. I later took the test again and improved my score even further, but I realized pretty far down the road to college how much I'd stressed myself out.

—*JOSEPH ANDA*
LITTLE ROCK, ARKANSAS
SAT/ACT SCORES: 2300
UNDECIDED

UPS AND DOWNS ... AND UPS

The days you get your scores are days you can never really forget. When I got my ACT score I was ecstatic. I never expected to do that well, so it caught me completely off guard. I felt that with my ACT score I might actually get into the schools that I had always wanted to get into. I called my parents and I was freaking out. I was so happy the rest of the day, I felt like nothing could bring me down.

The day I got my SAT scores was a lot different. The first time I got my scores back I was happy that I had at least gotten over 2000 and I was really happy with my Verbal score. But my Math score was low so I felt really bad about that. I figured that next time I would work harder and do better. But then when the scores came the second time around, I was shocked to see that my Verbal score went down, although my Math and Writing had gone up. Yeah, that was just a bad day. My dad was really disappointed about it. After all the prep that I had done, we expected a lot better. But after I got my ACT scores, I didn't even care about my SAT score anymore.

—*VIDYA SATHYAMOORTHY*
ROCKVILLE, MARYLAND
SAT/ACT SCORES: 2160/33
UNDECIDED

WHEN I GOT THE SCORE BACK, I was disappointed. I was hoping to get at least a 30. Three people at my school got a 30 and they were the talk
of the junior class. There was a special $500
scholarship for those students who received a 30
or better on the exam. I guess it was pride: I was
used to getting a lot of attention in high school
because I won most of the academic competitions. A lot of students made fun of me because I
didn't get a 30, even the ones who refused to
take the exam. But my score was still considered
above average, along with my 3.97 GPA, so I got
a full ride to college.

—*ZAKIA SIPP*
CHICAGO, ILLINOIS
SAT/ACT SCORES: 28
CHICAGO STATE UNIVERSITY

❝ When I actually saw the 35,
I jumped up and down and
ran around, shouting, 'I'm
going to college!' and I
called my two closest friends.
Needless to say, the entire
house was awake by
6 a.m. ❞

—*N.R.*
MEMPHIS, TENNESSEE
SAT/ACT SCORES: 1260/35
UNDECIDED

TAKING THE SAT AGAIN (AND AGAIN)

Many students take the SAT more than once. Here's what you need to know about retaking the test:

- There's no limit to how many times you can take the SAT. The consensus view is that colleges are fine with you taking the test at least three times. Some people claim that any more than that looks bad, although others seem to imply that there's no disadvantage to four or more tries. If you're focused on a particular college, you may want to call to ask them about their policy.

- Colleges will usually look at your best score. If you've taken the SAT, colleges will usually look to your best score as an indication of your ability. They're further motivated to do so because they want to report the highest possible SAT scores to those who rank colleges.

- You *can* improve your score. The less you prepared before the first time you took the test, the more likely you are to improve your score by trying again. On the other hand, if you've been studying like crazy and haven't improved your score in four separate attempts, you've probably reached or neared your peak.

I WAS RATHER NERVOUS and excited about getting my scores. I stayed up refreshing the College Board site until the scores were finally posted. After that, I spent a good deal of time thinking of ways to improve that score. I was actually shocked at my Math score: I'd expected at least a 760. And I beat myself up quite a bit about getting what I thought was an "abysmal" 710. But for critical reading and writing, I knew that I wasn't perfect and I knew how I was going to improve. This was my first crack at the SAT, and I took it as sort of a practice run since I had missed the PSAT.

—*Ashraf Eassa*
Windam, New Hampshire
SAT/ACT Scores: 2040
Massachusetts Institute of Technology

Random
SAT Wisdom

People have different opinions about the SAT and how important it should be as a component of the college admissions process. However, the students we spoke with all seemed to feel the same way, in retrospect, about this major life event: They're glad that it's over.

It doesn't seem that the SAT is going anywhere anytime soon. While more and more students are taking the ACT, and that exam is now accepted at just about every school, it's inevitable that you're probably going to have to take one of these two admissions tests if you want to go to college.

It's important that as you prepare for and eventually take the SAT or ACT, you keep everything in perspective. Test scores are important, but they're neither the only part of the college admissions process nor even the most important one. Your grades, your activities, your recommendations, and other factors will all play an important role in where you eventually go to school.

So whether you view the SAT as an obstacle or as an opportunity, remember that this is just one step on a long and winding road. And take to heart the advice you're given by those who have come before you—it won't be long, after all, before you're telling SAT war stories yourself.

IF YOU TRULY BELIEVE your SAT was scored incorrectly, you can pay $50 to have it scored by hand. My scores were a lot lower than I expected and I believed that the cause was eraser marks. I paid the $50 and it turned out that there was a scoring mistake.

—BRIAN WU
CORONA, CALIFORNIA
SAT/ACT SCORES: 2360
UNDECIDED

. . . .

I SEE WHY THEY NEED to standardize knowledge; however, I do not think that the knowledge tested on the SAT translates to success in college. Students who do well on the SAT are generally those who strive hard in school, and that's what colleges look for. In that respect I think that there's a correlation between doing well on the SAT and doing well in college.

—ISAAC
PHILADELPHIA, PENNSYLVANIA
SAT/ACT SCORES: 1300
MUHLENBERG COLLEGE

. . . .

AT FIRST I THOUGHT that colleges would accept me or reject me based mainly on my SAT score. What I didn't know was that the SAT wasn't the only thing that colleges were looking for.

—ANONYMOUS
BURBANK, CALIFORNIA
SAT/ACT SCORES: 870/19
PEPPERDINE UNIVERSITY

. . . .

A GOOD STRATEGY for reducing stress is tuning out people who harp on how hard the test is. It only intimidates you and fails to inspire the confidence that adequate preparation should bring.

—CLAIRE
EL PASO, TEXAS
SAT/ACT SCORES: 2280/33
CLEMSON UNIVERSITY

My mom wouldn't let me eat eggs the morning of the SAT because eggs look like zeros, so they're bad luck. It's an Asian thing.

—FEI ZANG
CAMARILLO, CALIFORNIA
WASHINGTON UNIVERSITY IN ST. LOUIS

I **TOOK THE SAT** **THREE TIMES** and scored best the time I took it in January. Most people say that the best time to take the test is January because that is when the curve is easier. The hardest curve is October. The reason for this is because in January you are competing with non-seniors.

—*M.C.*
KALAMAZOO, MICHIGAN
SAT/ACT SCORES: 2260/33
UNDECIDED

• • • • • • • •

I **THINK IT'S A MISCONCEPTION** that you'll be a better student after the SAT training and test. The SATs can't be studied by focusing on one thing. Thus you're not learning much from studying for the SATs. Specific study skills aren't required either, beyond simple self-discipline. The SATs are just something you have to get over with; you can't expect to gain anything out of it other than your score.

—*NAYOUNG*
PLAINSBORO, NEW JERSEY
CARNEGIE MELLON UNIVERSITY

• • • • • • • •

WHEN IT COMES TO THE SAT, always have a backup if you bomb on the test. I made sure I had references from teachers and mentors, an after-school job, high rankings in regional competitions, four extracurricular activities, community service, a B average, and a flawless essay. So when college admissions look at my SAT score, they will just say, "Oh, well she just had too much pressure from all her other academic commitments."

—*ANDREA PARKER*
CHICAGO, ILLINOIS
SAT/ACT SCORES: 890
SOUTHERN ILLINOIS UNIVERSITY, CARBONDALE

I was actually able to catch a nap between sections of the test. It was nice to have some rest in between.

—*ANONYMOUS*
CLAYTON, MISSOURI
SAT/ACT SCORES: 2060/32
UNDECIDED

ONCE THE **SAT** WAS OVER I felt really relieved and pretty proud of myself. It's just one test and it is not a barometer of intelligence in any way. However, I walked out of that room knowing I did well, and after all the preparation I had done in advance I felt pretty dignified. I was also very proud of myself when I received my score. It felt great to be successful at it.

—ANDREW MICHAEL RIZZI
BALDWIN, NEW YORK
SAT/ACT SCORES: 1390
SYRACUSE UNIVERSITY

• • • • • • • •

"Make sure you're wide-awake before the test. The essay part comes first, and trying to show off your dazzling vocabulary and brilliant thoughts at 7 a.m. can be a bit challenging."

—ANNIE STEPHENS
FORT THOMAS, KENTUCKY
WASHINGTON UNIVERSITY IN ST. LOUIS

• • • • • • • •

IF THE COLLEGE you are applying to requires multiple SAT II tests, don't take them in the same area. Even if you are going to be studying science, don't take one in chemistry, one in physics and one in biology. Try to make them diverse; take one in science, one in math, and one in history.

—BURTON DEWITT
MELVILLE, NEW YORK
SAT/ACT SCORES: 2080/32
RICE UNIVERSITY

I couldn't speak for two days after the test. I was totally spent.

—*Michal Rosenoer*
Corte Madera,
California
SAT/ACT
Scores: 2220
University of
California,
Berkeley

BE PREPARED TO WRITE a great college entry essay if you don't do well on the ACT. I didn't do well; I got a 23. I was an A student, on the honor roll, but all I was to a college admission board was a 23. ACT, SAT, and any other standardized test should be eliminated because everybody is not taught the same thing in every state and every city, at the same time, and by different teachers. Many students feel bad and question their academic ability if their score is not what they had hoped. Our other achievements like grades, extra curricular activities and our ambition should trump culturally biased standardized tests. My motto is, "Don't judge a student by his standardized test score."

—*Marquita Reese*
Chicago, Illinois
SAT/ACT Scores: 23
Chicago State University

• • • • • • • • •

IF YOU KNOW WHICH SCHOOLS you want to apply to, find out if they average your scores or if they will let you submit your best scores. You need to look into this if you are thinking about taking the test more than once. I took the SAT twice because most schools will let you choose your best score. A few schools will let you choose your best score from each section of the test. So if you took the test twice you could submit the Writing score from one of the tests and your Math score from another.

—*Aaron*
Beverly Hills, California
SAT/ACT Scores: 2150
University of California, Berkeley

CRITICISMS OF THE SAT

While the changes that took place in March of 2005 responded to a number of complaints about the SAT, the test remains under fire. The most frequent complaints about the SAT:

IT'S TOO LONG. Some think that the length of the test wears down students and overly rewards those who can remain focused throughout the long ordeal.

IT DOESN'T PREDICT COLLEGE SUCCESS. Critics believe that the SAT should be more content-oriented if it's going to demonstrate what students have learned in high school.

IT'S UNFAIR. Does the SAT discriminate against women and minorities? Some say that it does, pointing to lower scores among those groups.

IT FAVORS THE RICH. Wealthier parents are more able to afford expensive courses and private tutors to teach their children SAT strategies and methods.

I PERSONALLY DO NOT BELIEVE that the SAT prepared me for college, and found that the material I studied had no more to do with college classes than it did with high school. The SAT tests a very specific type of intelligence, one that is insensitive to economic and cultural differences, and not necessarily relevant to academic college performance. However, it is weighted very heavily in the college admissions process, so I do suggest that everyone take it extremely seriously. When the SAT was finally over, there is only one word that encompasses my feelings: relief.

—*BETH LORI WECKSELL*
GREAT NECK, NEW YORK
SAT/ACT SCORES: 1370
TUFTS UNIVERSITY

CREDITS

Page 8: www.azcentral.com/families/education/articles/0203edsat04facts-ON.htmAZCentral.com

Page 26: www.kaplan.com/aboutkaplan/pressreleases/archive/2002/June-27-sat_changes_0602.htm

Page 63: *Associated Press*, August 18, 2006, "Teenager in Kansas Scores Perfect on Both ACT, SAT"

Page 76: www.rediff.com/news/1999/jul/16us2.htm

SPECIAL THANKS

Thanks to our intrepid "headhunters" for going out to find so many respondents from around the country with interesting advice to share:

Jamie Allen, Chief Headhunter

Andrea Parker
Andrea Syrtash
Brandi Fowler
Daniel Nemet-Nejat
Jennifer Doll
Jessica Bloustein

John Nemo
Nancy Larson
Paula Andruss
Ruthann Spike
Staci Siegel

Thanks, too, to our editorial advisor Anne Kostick. And thanks to our assistant, Miri Greidi, for her yeoman's work at keeping us all organized. The real credit for this book, of course, goes to all the people whose experiences and collective wisdom make up this guide. There are too many of you to thank individually, but you know who you are.

CHECK OUT OTHER BOOKS
FROM HUNDREDS OF HEADS®

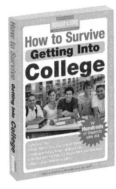

**HOW TO SURVIVE
GETTING INTO
COLLEGE**…by
Hundreds of
Students Who Did
(240 pages, $13.95)

ISBN-10: 1-933512-05-9
ISBN-13: 978-1933512-05-1

Book of the Year Award Winner, 2006
—FOREWORD MAGAZINE

"Everyone should have this book!"
—TODAY SHOW ANCHOR MEREDITH VIEIRA

"….a fun, fascinating read…"
—ABOUT.COM

"…chock-full of honest, heartfelt and often funny advice…"
—CHICAGO SUN-TIMES

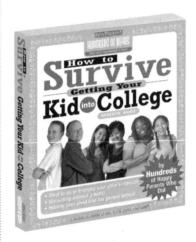

**HOW TO SURVIVE
GETTING YOUR
KID INTO
COLLEGE**…by
Hundreds of Happy
Parents Who Did
(240 pages, $14.95)

ISBN-10: 1-933512-11-3
ISBN-13: 978-1-933512-11-2

Today's college admissions game requires a team effort. Each year brings more applications, higher tuitions, and tougher admissions standards among competitive schools. In this book, hundreds of parents share their thoughts, strategies, struggles—even their failures—in navigating the college admissions process. Filled with tips, tricks, humor, and horror stories, it's a book to help parents help their kids succeed.

Hundreds of successful college students and graduates share their wisdom, stories, tips, and advice on how to get high grades, choose the right major, manage your time, study smart, stay motivated, avoid stress, find the best teachers and courses, form important relationships, and graduate—happily—at the top of your class.

HOW TO GET A's IN COLLEGE
Hundreds of Student-Tested Tips
(240 pages, $14.95)

ISBN-10: 1-933512-08-3
ISBN-13: 978-1933512-08-2

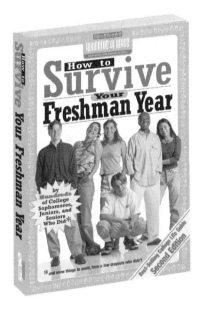

HOW TO SURVIVE YOUR FRESHMAN YEAR...by Hundreds of Sophomores, Juniors, and Seniors Who Did
(256 pages, $14.95)

ISBN-10: 1-933512-04-0
ISBN-13: 978-1933512-04-4

"This book proves that all of us are smarter than one of us."

—JOHN KATZMAN
FOUNDER AND CEO, PRINCETON REVIEW

"Voted in the Top 40 Young Adults Nonfiction books."

—PENNSYLVANIA SCHOOL LIBRARIANS ASSOCIATION

"This cool new book ... helps new college students get a head start on having a great time and making the most of this new and exciting experience."

—COLLEGE OUTLOOK

WHAT THE CRITICS ARE SAYING ABOUT HUNDREDS OF HEADS®:

"The next 'Dummies' or 'Chicken Soup' … offers funny but blunt advice from thousands across America who've walked some of life's rougher roads."

—DEMOCRAT AND CHRONICLE (ROCHESTER, NEW YORK)

"Colorful bits of advice … So simple, so entertaining, so should have been my million-dollar idea."

—THE COURIER-JOURNAL (LOUISVILLE, KENTUCKY)

"The series … could be described as 'Chicken Soup for the Soul' meets 'Worst Case Scenario.'"

—ATLANTA BUSINESS CHRONICLE

"Entertaining and informative series takes a different approach to offering advice...Think 'Chicken Soup' meets 'Zagats'..."

—THE SACRAMENTO BEE

TELL US YOUR STORY™

... and join Hundreds of Heads®.

Become one of the hundreds of smart and funny voices of experience whose collected wisdom makes our books so great. Survived a life experience and learned a lesson from it? Keep a mental list of do's and don'ts? Know an amazing story that happened to a friend or relative? Tell us about it. Share your advice, get published, and join the hundreds of contributors to the series.

Click on **www.hundredsofheads.com** to:

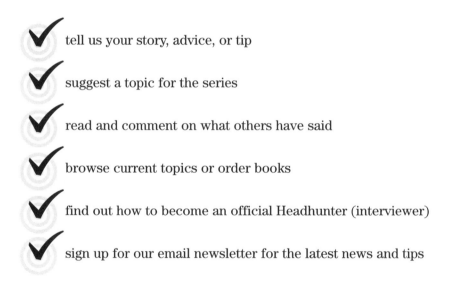

tell us your story, advice, or tip

suggest a topic for the series

read and comment on what others have said

browse current topics or order books

find out how to become an official Headhunter (interviewer)

sign up for our email newsletter for the latest news and tips

www.hundredsofheads.com

ABOUT THE EDITOR

JAY BRODY is a full-time college admissions counselor based in Chicago. He works with dozens of families each year on applications, essays, interviewing, scholarships, SATs, and ACTs. In addition, Brody manages a number of SAT courses and tutoring programs. Brody is the author of a popular admissions essay guide available in bookstores and used in public school programs. He has appeared on national television to discuss issues concerning the SAT and learning disabilities. He earned an English degree from Williams College and a law degree from Harvard.